Lucy: I think about sex during the day, staring at my computer screen, while I'm supposed to be writing a grant. Sometimes I call Dana up at work, she picks up the phone, I say, "I'll meet you at home in fifteen minutes," which drives her crazy, especially if she can't come home. "I'll meet you at home in fifteen minutes, and I'm going to rip off your clothes and throw you down on the couch, and I'm going to eat your pussy. That's what I'm having for lunch."

Sometimes she gets mad, "Shhh," she says, "I'm not alone in the office," which instantly inspires me to new and greater heights. "They don't know I'm talking about pulling off your underwear," and so on. She blushes and giggles and says, "I told you, don't do that! I can't leave the office right now, so I'm going to go around wet all afternoon." She cracks me up. Here we've been together nearly twenty years and she's still blushing and giggling.

So then she says, "You're too wicked. Don't ever call me at work again and whisper to me like that." But she doesn't hang up on me, of course.

LESBIAN SEX:

AN ORAL HISTORY

BY
SUSAN E.
JOHNSON

THE NAIAD PRESS, INC.
1996

Printed in the United States of America on acid-free paper
First Edition

Editor: Lisa Epson
Cover designer: Bonnie Liss (Phoenix Graphics)
Typesetter: Sandi Stancil

Library of Congress Cataloging-in-Publication Data

Johnson, Susan E., 1940–
    Lesbian sex : an oral history / by Susan E. Johnson.
        p.   cm.
    ISBN 1-56280-142-2
    1. Lesbians—Sexual behavior.   2. Lesbians—Interviews.
I. Title.
HQ75.5.J64   1996
306.76'63—dc20   96-18989
                                                            CIP

For Connie

Thank You

Acknowledgments

My most sincere thanks to the fourteen women who shared with me the intimate details of their sexual lives and thus made available to all of us the unique material that is *Lesbian Sex: An Oral History*. Sex is a source of pleasure, but sometimes it is a source of pain as well. These women courageously told me the whole story, and I am immensely grateful.

I also want to thank

My partner, Connie Wolfe, and my friend, Gretchen Legler, both of whom read the manuscript, made many helpful suggestions, and helped me keep everything within the bounds of good taste . . . more or less;

My transcribers, Carol Van Dyke, Patricia Huling, and Cindy Riche, who transformed tapes into print with such care;

Barbara Grier, Donna McBride, and the other fine women of Naiad Press, whose bizarre idea this was;

Lisa Epson, my meticulous copy editor; and

My friends, who helped with this project in a variety of important ways: Bucky Dennerlein, Myth Denzel, Connie Huey, Linda Imle, Jackie Jones, Lisa Moorehead, Holly Morris, Sandra Jo Palm, Jan Pickard, Sharon Reed, and Anglie Slingluff. And special thanks to Ruth Mathes, who saw me through it all.

About the Author

Susan E. Johnson, Ph.D. (University of Wisconsin, Madison) has been a lesbian for almost forty years and a sociologist nearly as long. She is the author of two books about long-term lesbian couples: *Staying Power: Long Term Lesbian Couples* (Naiad Press, 1990), which reports her nationwide study of 108 lesbian couples who have been together ten years or more; and *For Love and For Life* (Naiad Press, 1995), intimate in-depth portraits of ten long-term couples. She is also the author of *When Women Played Hardball* (Seal Press, 1994), a revealing portrait of ten-year-old fan Susan's heroes, the women who played professional baseball in "a league of their own."

Susan lives with her partner in Anchorage, Alaska. Although she continues her personal and professional research into lesbian sex, she has yet to try everything described in this book.

CONTENTS

LESBIAN SEX:

AN ORAL HISTORY

BY
SUSAN E.
JOHNSON

Preface

For a few months seventeen years ago I was in love with a woman with whom I made love only once. She had just broken up with her partner and had been living alone for only a short time; her apartment felt as if she were camping out there, a paisley-print sheet covering her window, one aluminum saucepan and mismatched plates and coffee mugs stocking her kitchen, her mattress lying on the floor. But carefully mounted on red poster board and hanging on her wall was this poem her partner had given her:

> LOVING WOMEN IS...
> Taste beyond pleasure
> And pleasure beyond touch
> And touch beyond feeling
> And feeling beyond senses
> And senses beyond consciousness
> And consciousness beyond reality
> And reality beyond madness
> And madness beyond belief.

I copied this poem on a three-by-five piece of cheap notepaper and have carried it folded up in my wallet ever since, the paper softening with age, the edges growing ragged. The author is S. Rhue, the creator of what I thought was the most erotic, the most sensual, the sexiest thing I had ever read. And I still do.

I have this poem with me everywhere I go. Sometimes I sort through my credit cards and airline mileage cards searching for it, needing to read these delicious words, to taste them in my mouth. Sometimes I come upon the poem unexpectedly; I catch my breath and am momentarily disoriented, startled to be plunged without warning into consciousness of my own desire.

The "Loving Women Is..." poem is my totem, my emblem of membership in the clan Lesbian, the connection with my own passion I want near me always. It is a symbol of the importance for me of being lesbian and being sexual, an identity and a behavior whose complex and intimate intertwinings are the subject of *Lesbian Sex: An Oral History*.

Lesbian Sex: An Oral History reveals the stories of fourteen women who allowed me to interview them about the most intimate details of their sexual lives. The book is full of graphic details; you will be left in no doubt about who did what to whom. It is an explicit book.

But *Lesbian Sex: An Oral History* is a more profound

and more complex book as well. These women tell us not only what they do, but how they feel about what they do, what sex means to them in the context of their lives, how their sexual behavior affects their lesbian identity, how what they do in bed affects who they are. It is a book not only about sex, but about sexuality.

This book presents the stories of a variety of women. The fourteen lesbians interviewed are geographically diverse, one or more growing up on the east and west coasts, in the mountain states, and in the midwest; eleven are Caucasian, two are African-American, and one Chicana; one is deaf; all of the women are now middle class but several were raised working class; they come from all three western religious traditions, Protestant, Catholic, and Jewish; the youngest is eighteen years old, the oldest eighty-two; and their sexual practices range from vanilla to rum raisin to Heath bar crunch.

There are, of course, many similarities among them. They all think sex is important, sometimes important enough — at least for the ex-Catholic women — to warrant religious imagery. They describe lesbian sex with phrases like "worship of the body" and "blessing the body."

Sex is important for lesbians we may secretly think are not sexual at all. If you believe, for instance, the myth that old lesbians aren't sexual, here is eighty-two-year-old Lynn, who had a "torrid affair" (her words) when she was seventy-nine with a woman half her age. Or if you think differently-abled lesbians aren't sexual, read about Hannah, who is deaf, who has been sexual with several previous partners, and who is now enjoying an eleven-year relationship with Kay, her hearing partner.

Many of the women share a passionate interest in kissing. Lynn says, "A good kisser is really to be treasured." Kay, Hannah's partner, says, "I love kissing. I think kissing is the most wonderful invention."

All the women believe talking and sex go together,

though how they put them together differs. Crystal emphasizes the negotiations necessary before S/M play can begin. For Grace, talking helps heal past sexual abuse.

And, of course, some like to talk just for the turn-on and the fun of it. Hannah, for instance, who tells stories to Kay while they're having sex, says, "I know when to rush the story through, or when to slow the story down!"

I was struck by the fact that several women described their first sexual experience with another woman using the same metaphor: They spoke of "coming home." Hazel, a fifty-four-year-old woman, who eventually became sexual with a woman she had been in love with for many years, says of the experience, "I felt like I'd come home; I was being who I was intended to be."

There is also, of course, great variety among these women. They became lesbians at different stages of their lives. Lynn, now eighty-two, became a lesbian at age forty-six, after twenty-five years of marriage. Grace, now thirty-six, can document her lesbianism back to the age of ten, with love letters to Miss Thomas, her fifth-grade teacher.

The women who are partnered have different philosophies about monogamy. Kay and Hannah have agreed to be monogamous because, as Kay explains, "I believe strongly that relationships do not do well when people are having sex with other people outside of the relationship." Hazel feels differently about it and has concluded, "Being primary with one woman and sexual with another woman feels like figuring out what hand you've been dealt and doing the best you can with it."

The women are also different in their attitudes about and experience with particular sexual practices. Let me illustrate with just one example, the matter of dildos.

Grace's partner, Lindy, expresses an interest in dildos, but also considerable embarrassment about the whole idea of buying, much less using, one. She worries, "I'm a lesbian and not supposed to be interested in the man thing." Laura, in contrast, is the co-owner of a sex toy store, helps customers select from among ninety — I counted them — different styles of dildos, and says of herself, "I have access to all of these, but I, of course, have my favorites."

In *Lesbian Sex: An Oral History* we come to know all these lesbians as complex women. They tell us about their sexual histories, what they were taught as children, what they did as adolescents. They share their first attractions and the first time they were sexual with a woman. They recount the relationships they've enjoyed and those they've struggled through, and the connections they've made that were too short to call relationships. They tell us of their awkward moments and their hilariously funny times. They relate stories of problems and anguish, of excitement and joy, of tantalizing sensations and heart-stopping thrills. And throughout, they tell us of love, and of how love and lust are intertwined.

The material in *Lesbian Sex: An Oral History* was gathered through in-depth, in-person interviews conducted during 1995 and 1996. Typically I would go to the woman's home, settle down at her kitchen table, and talk with her for two or three hours about the details of her sexual experience. The interviews were taped, the tapes transcribed, and the profiles written from these verbatim transcripts, with some rearranging of content and editing only for clarity. The names, locations, and other distinguishing facts about the actual women who participated in this study were changed to protect their anonymity.

The interviews were based on a twenty-page interview schedule that included a wide variety and a huge number of questions. There was never time to ask all of these questions of every woman, but some proved to be so central that they formed the backbone of the interview. I would like to share these most significant questions with you, and have thus included them at the end of the book, in the section Let's Talk About Sex. It is my hope that you will take these questions, get together with your partner and/or friends, and try to answer some or all of them, to share with one another the intimacy and joy of your sexual lives.

I have chosen to present these fourteen women's stories beginning with Lynn, the oldest at age eighty-two, and progressing in order of age, from oldest to youngest, until we hear at the end from Jane, who is nineteen. This allows you to orient these women's stories within the context of our ongoing lesbian and gay history.

We are all captives of our time in history, and thus much of what we know and feel, enjoy and fear, is born out of the intersection of our own private life with the public life around us. How we define our lesbian identity, how we express our lesbian sexuality, how we understand our lesbian selves, all are importantly influenced by when we were born, when we came out, when we first made love to a woman. Each woman's life is grounded in her own time, and it is thus that she can best be understood.

Lynn, for instance, was fifty-seven in 1969, the year of the Stonewall Resistance, the beginning of our open struggle for gay rights. By that time Lynn had already survived twenty-five years of marriage and a divorce and was two years into mourning the death of Margery, the woman with whom she had shared a long-term and closeted relationship for nine years.

Hazel, now fifty-four, in 1969 was just ending her first relationship with a woman, one that had lasted seven years. She was firm in her lesbian identity and was moving into her serially semimonogamous period, a time when she would explicitly experiment with creating rules for her sexual behavior.

Rita, now forty-five, was nineteen, and making the decision to put aside her attractions for women. She learned how to control men, married, and became the mother of three, fulfilling the path laid out for a traditional Chicana. It was not until two years ago, twenty-five years after Stonewall, that she reclaimed her lesbian identity.

Thirty-six-year-old Grace, on the other hand, while only eleven in 1969, was already in love with Miss Thomas, and a whole year earlier had told her entire fifth-grade class "I'm a homosexual, and this is love I am feeling, and it's fine."

And nineteen-year-old Jane, who took her girlfriend to her high-school senior prom, hadn't been born yet; she is leaving her mother's home and going away to college with a female lover twenty-seven years after Stonewall.

Two notes of caution before you begin. This book explores the stories of fourteen individual lesbians in all the intimate detail that an in-depth study can offer, but in no way are the women in this book representative of anything more than themselves and their own experience. It is an oral history of these particular women, all of whom identify themselves as lesbians, with the exception of one young woman who identifies herself as a dyke. *Lesbian Sex: An Oral History* does not purport to be about all lesbians or lesbians in general.

It is also likely that not everyone you come to know in this book and everything they do will meet with your personal approval. These women articulate diverse sexual practices and points of view, and thus there should be something here to comfort and something to titillate and something to offend every reader. The goal is to make explicit and available to you the vitality and variety of lesbian sexual experience. It is not to suggest that, because these women do or think or feel *X* and *Y* and *Z*, you should too. It is my hope that you will take *Lesbian Sex: An Oral History* as an opportunity to expand what you know about lesbian sexuality, as a motivation to become more open and curious about your own sexual life, and as an invitation to enrich your own sexual pleasure.

We lesbians are a sexual minority and as such are regarded by much of our society as sexual outlaws or deviants or perverts, decidedly not-normal. I suppose, then, it is not surprising that some of us worry about whether or not we are normal, normal as compared to other lesbians, that is. This worry seems useless to me because we cannot hope to find the "normal lesbian" to pattern ourselves after; she doesn't exist. Instead we are fated to enjoy one of the things that lured us into becoming lesbians in the first place, the opportunity to create our own unique sexual lives, lives not imitative of those we see around us.

One woman worried during the interview about whether or not what she was doing with her partner was okay. She was feeling self-conscious and ashamed, as if maybe she was a bad lesbian. She asked me, "What's it like normally?"

"Oh," I assured her, "there isn't any 'normally.' Wait 'til you read the book!"

Lynn

"People who say you lose your sex drive
the older you get don't know what
they're talking about."

Carol was a very, very lovely black woman, nearly forty years younger than me. We had been to a basketball game together — we were both Chicago Bulls fans — and she drove me back to my apartment. I was saying goodnight to her, and all of a sudden she grabbed me and kissed me. I was so startled I couldn't think of anything to say except, "Oh my god, this is wonderful." And she said, "Well, in that case, you better invite me in."

I was seventy-nine at the time. I'm so deeply grateful

that I had the time with Carol that I did. That was such
a delight and such a bonus. A torrid affair was something
I wasn't expecting at my age.

Lynn is a tiny, eighty-two-year-old white woman with
short thinning hair and an elfish look. She and her puppy,
Fritz, whom she had rescued from the pound only a week
before our interview, opened the door to welcome me into
her small, sparsely furnished home in a tidy working-class
neighborhood northwest of Chicago. Though Lynn held a
mid-level professional job for a period of her life, she is
now dependent on scant resources, helped materially by her
sister who, Lynn proudly told me, has been a lesbian all
her life.

Lynn was dressed comfortably in sneakers, slacks, and
a sweatshirt. She immediately offered me a cup of coffee,
walking slowly to and from the kitchen, a bit bent over,
carefully balancing both mugs so as not to spill. Once we
were comfortably seated, she favored me with the first of
many beaming smiles, the prelude to several hours of
animated talk. She began at the beginning, with her
childhood.

Lynn: I was a bottle-fed baby, and my parents thought
as long as I wanted the bottle, why I could have it. So up
'til the time I was about four years old, I went to bed
with a bottle. By the time I was about three, I remember
distinctly, I had discovered other uses for it. I would slide
the bottle down along my body and rub the nipple against
my clitoris.

Susan: That's very creative.

Lynn: Well, you work with what you've got!

One night my parents noticed that the nipple on my

bottle had just been chewed to pieces. They decided I needed a new one, but the drugstore was closed; I would have to sleep without my bottle. I put myself to sleep crying. They didn't know why, but I knew why. And from then on I used my hands instead.

They say that kids can't remember things, but I have many memories from when I was young. I was raised with two of my boy cousins. When I was about six or seven, the oldest — he was twelve — decided that we'd play these games. He was rough, and I didn't like it. But I wanted to be as big as they were, and I thought, Well, if that's what you do when you grow up, why I'll do it. My other cousin, who was ten, was gentler, and he didn't really hurt me, but the twelve-year-old did. I just sort of knew about sex from then on.

Susan: Did they actually put their penises in you?

Lynn: Yeah. I think so. I'm not just sure.

Susan: Sounds kind of scary.

Lynn: Yeah. But I think most kids about that age do something like that. As we grew up I was never close to the older one. But with the younger one I was very close. As a matter of fact, when I was in nurses training, we even had sex together a couple of times. But it wasn't anything we were really going to pursue.

I was engaged to a young man in high school. I thought I was going to marry him, but I just couldn't bring myself to, somehow.

Susan: Were you sexual with him?

Lynn: Yeah. And I didn't like it. So I got out of that engagement, went into nurses training and [she pauses delicately] well, I'm afraid I sort of slept around before I was married. With maybe five or six men.

Susan: Was there anything fun or exciting about it?

Lynn: I was searching all this time. And I wasn't finding what I was looking for.

I finally settled on the young man I married. I was twenty-four years old, and it was 1936. At first I thought I was in love with him simply because he was very sweet. He wasn't rough or mean, and I thought I loved him. And I thought, Well, maybe it'll be different with him. But it wasn't.

Susan: You mean maybe being sexual would be different?

Lynn: Yeah, because, unlike the rest of them, I didn't sleep with Paul until we were married and because, believe it or not, he was a virgin. I think he married me in part because I was a more experienced woman [she laughs quite delightedly].

We had a lot of interests in common, and he was a very persuasive type. Our social life was quite interesting because he worked for *The Chicago Tribune* and was personal friends with our Illinois senators and representatives in Washington. I was forced into the role of being a hostess. I didn't always like that role, but it was important to him, and there's a certain charm to meeting some of these people that you read about in the paper all the time. It was fun too. I had to wear different type clothes, the whole thing. It was like another life.

I think if we hadn't had our daughter, though, I might have left before I did. Although I don't know. You can't tell about those things.

Lynn stayed married to Paul for twenty-five years. Three years before they were divorced, Lynn had met Margery. Lynn was forty-six years old and the country was just moving out of the prosperous and solidly conservative 1950s into the experimental and rebellious 1960s.

Lynn: Paul didn't want me to work. But by the time our daughter was getting ready for college I got tired of being a housewife. I worked in a bookstore, and Margery and her husband were customers of mine. When the bookstore closed, she was helpful in finding me a job at Northwestern University, where I worked for fifteen years as head of an editorial office associated with the biology department.

During the move from the bookstore to the university, I saw more and more of Margery, and by 1960 we had decided that we wanted to be together. It took about two years, but finally I got my divorce, she left her husband, and we moved in together.

Susan: Had you and Margery become lovers by this time?

Lynn: Oh yes.

Susan: So, what felt different about being in love with a woman?

Lynn: I felt like I'd come home.

Lynn is a lesbian who, like many others, has had considerable sexual experience with men. I asked her to reflect on what she thought were the differences between having sex with a man and having sex with a woman.

Lynn: Through twenty-five years of marriage, and my experimenting with other men before I was married, I never, ever had an orgasm until I met Margery.

Susan: Can you remember that first orgasm?

Lynn: Yes!

Susan: Can you describe it?

Lynn: Well, it's been a long time, but I just know that I thought, "Oh my god, this is what it's all about." And it was the same thing for dear Margery. She'd been married and had had numerous affairs, and had never felt an orgasm with any of them.

Susan: So what do you think the difference is?

Lynn: I think we're born lesbians. And I think it's genetic too. I don't think any real, honest-to-god lesbian could ever enjoy sex with a man. I don't believe in these bisexual things that they talk about because it doesn't make sense to me.

Susan: You mean you don't think a person can be as interested in both sexes?

Lynn: I don't think so. I think that's sort of stupid. I don't think our genes and all would work that way. I think it has to be one or the other.

Susan: Do you think the pleasure you have with women that you don't have with men is because a woman makes love to another woman differently than a man does? Or do you think it's because of your feelings for her?

Lynn: I think it's the extent of the feeling between the two of us. But it's also the way lesbians approach love. Men: foreplay, forget it! They just do their thing and then they fall asleep and that's it. That's not how it's supposed to be, but it is the way it happens. And I sampled enough, particularly when I was in nurses training, to realize that it wasn't just one man. It was all. But at the time, I didn't know that there was anything else out there for me.

Susan: How important would you say sex was to your relationship with Margery?

Lynn: It was a part of it. If the sex hadn't been good, none of the rest of it would've been good. But we were both quiet people and were content to do quiet things. We lived for seven years on a boat moored at the Evanston marina on Lake Michigan. And we would take our boat out on the lake sometimes and enjoy watching the other boats.

Of course we didn't know any other lesbian couples. Well, we knew of one couple, but we didn't dare say anything to them because they were in the same department. On campus to be lesbian or gay was sudden death.

Susan: Can you compare your sexual life with Margery, when you were closeted, with your sexual life now?

Lynn: I think being out you feel freer somehow. Because when you're closeted there is a certain tension to knowing that you don't dare put your arm around someone or hold their hand, you know. All of your impulses have to be tamped down and channeled into the places where they'll fit. And if you're out, that's different.

Susan: So what would you say is better about the sex?

Lynn: It's more spontaneous I think. Or . . . maybe just old age does it!

Susan: What did you like to do when you and Margery made love?

Lynn: Well, I liked the whole bit.

Susan: Did you like oral sex?

Lynn: Oh yes! Absolutely. I think that's part of it.

Susan: Both doing it and receiving it?

Lynn: Yeah.

Susan: And how about penetration?

Lynn: Well, we never used anything except just our hands.

Susan: And did you like that?

Lynn: Mmmhmm [she's nodding yes]. Though it was more of a clitoral stimulation.

Susan: Have you ever had a vaginal orgasm?

Lynn: [Long pause. Lynn is caught between her loyalty to Margery and her commitment to the truth.] Just once, but it was with Carol just a few years ago, not with Margery.

Susan: Were either you or Margery more butch or more femme?

Lynn: No. We never thought of that. In neither one of my relationships has that come up. It's been mutual.

Susan: How often would you and Margery have sex?

Lynn: Two or three times a week. Though Margery was sick a lot, and sometimes it dwindled because of that. She felt bad about it.

Margery had a tricky heart, a very weird pulse. And she never could get her doctor to really pay attention to it. So one day her heart went into fibrillation and just went. I came home to the cabin cruiser and discovered her. That was rough.

The only person that I could really talk to about it — because I wasn't out then at all — was my sister. She stayed with me for a few days, but couldn't stay any longer. So I had no support. I just had to get through my grief by myself.

Matter of fact, it took me almost twenty years to forgive Margery for dying. But I finally did. I know that if she had lived, we would've still been together.

Lynn suggested a break at this point, so we could shake off our awareness of the sadness of interrupted lives and love lost, the mood of mourning that had fallen upon us. We walked into the kitchen to refill our coffees; Lynn produced cookies and gave some attention to Fritz, and we returned refreshed to our places in the living room.

Susan: So tell me more about Carol, about your affair three years ago.

Lynn: That was a lovely affair. It was like something out of a book, really.

Susan: Tell me what happened after that first goodnight kiss.

Lynn: That was all it took! We went inside and first

we did a lot of smoochin'! And then I asked her how old she was. Well, she was barely forty-one, and I was seventy-nine. I said, "Oh boy, there's too much difference in our ages. I don't think we ought to start something; one of us will get hurt." And she said, "No, no, no. I've always gone for older people. You're what I want."

Later she did meet someone younger. But I had noticed that her relationships only lasted about two years anyway. I don't regret a minute of it, though, because they were fairy-tale years, those two years we spent together. It was a gift.

Susan: You said it was torrid. Was it torrid?

Lynn: It was torrid!

Susan: Tell me about it.

Lynn: Well, people who say that you lose your sex drive the older you get don't know what they're talking about because you never lose it. Never. I was more than pleasantly surprised to see that I could react at seventy-nine and eighty with as much fire as I had as a younger woman.

Susan: You said you had a vaginal orgasm with Carol. What happened?

Lynn: Well, she had this vibrator thing, and that was my undoing.

Susan: Tell me about it.

Lynn: Well...it...it... Really, I don't have the vocabulary to describe what it did.

Susan: Did she have the vibrator inside you?

Lynn: Yeah. It precipitated this terrific feeling. It was like an explosion! It was weird, I'll tell you that.

Susan: Can you describe it for me?

Lynn: It was more colors than anything else. And I broke out in just terrific perspiration, and it was like my

whole body just clamped down real hard. Carol was much
more skilled than Margery and I had been, and she
was . . . well . . . just different.

Susan: Did you make love a lot with her and the
vibrator?

Lynn: We didn't use the vibrator very often. But we
made love a lot. For two years we made love on a daily
basis, and then it got so it would be maybe three or four
times a week.

Susan: Can you remember any scene with Carol that
was particularly funny?

Lynn: Well, she was an avid Bingo player, and her
brother would sometimes take her to these big expensive
Bingo places. I didn't go because I didn't feel like I could
afford to play in that league. So one night when she came
home I was already asleep. She turned on the light and
showered me with bills. She had won seven hundred fifty
dollars. We sat there like ghouls, laughing and throwing
around this money. There were lots of fun things I did
with Carol.

Susan: Can you think of anything sexual that was
funny?

Lynn: No. That was too intense. There wasn't anything
funny about it. Sex was a whole 'nother thing.

Susan: Can you remember some very favorite time that
you made love with her?

Lynn: [Long pause] No, I see it in my mind now as
just a progression of days and nights.

Susan: Did you make love at night, or during the day,
or . . . ?

Lynn: Any time the mood struck us!

Susan: Did you make love just in bed or . . . ?

Lynn: Any place! Just wherever we were in the house.

Susan: Did she usually start things, or did you?

Lynn: It was mutual.

Susan: Did you like to talk while you were having sex?

Lynn: Oh yes! It was just spontaneous. I never knew what I was going to say.

Susan: What might you say?

Lynn: Her name, or "Oh my god," things like that.

Susan: Would you say what you'd like her to do?

Lynn: Yeah.

Susan: And did you make noise? Were you loud?

Lynn: Oh yes! Don't we all? [She pauses, remembering something else.]

It was exciting! She was a big woman, perhaps five-foot-six or so. And I'm just four-foot-eleven. And she was husky. She cracked a couple of my ribs once. She grabbed me up and swung me around and I felt this — oh god — and went to the doctor. Sure enough I had two cracked ribs.

So we had to take it easy for a while.

I was out to my doctor and told him, "My lover grabbed me up and swung me around," and he said, "I hope she never bites you." [Gales of laughter.]

Much later in the discussion, when talk had turned to Lynn's health, she almost incidentally told me about having undergone a radical mastectomy four years earlier. We talked about cancer for a while and some other serious health problems Lynn has had. Then I returned the discussion to the timing of her breast cancer diagnosis.

Susan: Did your mastectomy happen after you and Carol broke up?

Lynn: No, it happened just as we were getting together. I knew that I had this lump, but I was pretending like I didn't. The minute she discovered it she said, "You are going to a doctor." So I did. We had been lovers for about six months when I had my surgery. She was a nurse too, and helped take care of the drains and things. I would get all sorts of funny reactions in my body, whether from the surgery or the hormones. The first year was pretty rugged.

Susan: Now while all this is going on you're having this wild sex life with her?

Lynn: [Laughing.] Yeah, except for the times when I was flat on my back trying to combat my illness.

Susan: Was losing a breast traumatic in terms of your body image or how you felt about yourself sexually?

Lynn: Yes. And it would have been much more so had it not been for Carol. I give her full credit for the fact that I was able to overcome that, because never by word or look did she indicate that it made any difference in her feelings, and I believed her. I'm so grateful. I can't imagine anyone having the kind of support that I did.

Susan: Well, you were also able to take in that love and support. You could have been so depressed that it wouldn't have mattered what Carol did.

Lynn: Well, I guess I have a will to survive too.

Lynn has not had a sexual partner since she and Carol broke up. I asked her to tell me what her sex life is like without a lover.

Susan: Do you like to fantasize about sexual things?

Lynn: I think I take it out in my reading. I think I've read every lesbian novel that's come out, and I've got most of them, and I read them over and over again. I use that instead of fantasies.

Susan: Do you like erotica or pornography?

Lynn: I don't like what you'd call pornography, but I've got some lovely lesbian videos.

Lynn's extensive library of lesbian novels includes her current favorite, *Forever* by Evelyn Kennedy. Lynn says, "She was a former nun, and her books are good." Another book I picked up says on the back, "To each of us who finds the wisdom to listen to her heart and gathers the courage to follow it." Her lesbian videos include *Desert Hearts*, and *Long Awaited Pleasure* ("the lesbian love story you've always wanted to see"), and *Love Game* ("Will tennis star Dana Johnson ever find true love?").

Susan: What about the physical part of your sex life. Do you masturbate now?

Lynn: I take care of myself from time to time. I just know that I've got cravings, and at this point in my life there's one way I can sort of tamp them down, and that's all it amounts to.

I masturbate because the need is there and I've got to get rid of it. I think it's just going through the motions. But having sex ... well, it takes somebody else actively participating in the deed to give it its true worth.

Susan: And what do you think that true worth is?

Lynn: The wonderful euphoria that you feel when you're through. I just ... well ... I feel complete. [Lynn's face softens and a small, sweet smile appears.]

I think that the part of the sex act that is really wonderful is the kissing part. A good kisser is really to be treasured.

Susan: Is kissing your favorite thing to do?

Lynn: Well, kissing is a great part of it, yeah. But I think the stimulation of my clitoris is the crux of the matter. [The smile has become a mischievous grin.]

Susan: Which you discovered when you were three years old.

Lynn: And I've never deviated from that! I'm consistent, at least.

Susan: So what role do you think sex has played in your life?

Lynn: Lesbian sex has been the happiest part of my life. I just wonder now why it took me so long to figure it out.

Hazel

"If I'm not being sexual, I feel like I'm in
the closet again."

Between 1976 and 1980 I was sexual with a lot of
women, some totally inappropriate. Some of these
connections were relationships and some were not. I was
trying to figure out for myself what my ground rules were,
what things would feel good and ethical, right and
satisfying to me.

Rule number one I was trying to explore was that, just
because a relationship is casual doesn't mean it can't be
really caring and serious. I don't think I was into sport

23

fucking or sex for its own sake, but now that I look back at it, I was certainly into experimenting. There was one person I had no idea what her name was, and somebody else who was even a little more disastrous, one-night-almost stands you could say. It was research, but not in a calculating way; I tried to be genuine.

Rule number two I discovered was, I don't think women do casual.

Hazel is a fifty-four-year-old woman who works in Milwaukee but lives to be outside the city, hiking and canoeing and cross-country skiing. She wore a red, blue, and green plaid flannel shirt, khaki pants, and hiking boots to the interview. She is short, perhaps five feet three, and round, with very short, straight, reddish-brown hair, evidence of her 100 percent Irish heritage. She thinks analytically more easily than concretely and talks fast, words and ideas tumbling over each other in her haste to say what she means in all its abstract complexity.

Although Hazel was sexually active by the mid-seventies, when feminism was suggesting women create new, unconventional models for their behavior, she had not always been so daring. As a child she, like other intellectual children, was living her life through books.

Hazel: I learned the facts of life from reading *The Brothers Karamazov*. There was something in the novel about what body parts went where and, more importantly, there was this intensity and this incredible, lurid, nervous feeling that the adults in the book had about it. I was interested in the intensity and the guilt, but not the sex. I just thought, Ohhh, okay, I get it, about the sex.

As a kid I don't have any memories of sexual feelings. The heterosexual thing never seemed to have anything personal to do with me. At some point in high school I knew we were supposed to be dating, but I wasn't really interested. If there was some big-deal occasion, I'd go out with one of the official smart boys who wasn't really interested in sex either.

Susan: Did you have crushes on boys? On girls?

Hazel: On girls, but I managed to be very naive about it for a long time. The first time I was attracted to a woman was in college, but I was still slow to think about it in a sexual category. Which was kind of good, because Nancy and I got to have this intense friendship, a kind of innocence that would be hard to have now. Somehow I knew it was about sex, and I still didn't think about it. I would have dreams about *other* people being lesbians.

Susan: What do you think was good about maintaining your innocence?

Hazel: The culture at the time was really threatening, and I wasn't ready to take on those battles. Being innocent kept me a child longer, it kept me from getting into situations I don't think I would have been ready to deal with.

Toward the end of my senior year in college I was becoming more aware. I knew I was in love with Nancy, but I didn't make the further connection about being a lesbian. And she was saying things like, "We should go build a cabin together." But she couldn't say it seriously, it was a kidding around kind of thing.

And then she got married. I knew she wasn't in love with her husband. By this time I was in graduate school in New England, and that was when I caught on. Once I realized I was a lesbian, it was not terrifying to me; it just made sense. It was politically enlightening too, because I thought, If the culture has lied to me about this, what else have they lied about!

I would go to some of the lesbian bars in New York and — even though I was crossing class lines and even though they were scary to me — I felt these really tough working-class girls were gutsy and were my allies.

My relationship with Nancy continued even though she was married, and we started getting close to being sexual. She was rubbing my back once, very tenderly — her husband was asleep upstairs — and she said, "This doesn't mean we're lesbians, you know." And I said, "Well, sure it does!" At the time the whole myth of what being a lesbian was was so skewed that she just wasn't ready to buy all that. She wasn't denying she loved me, or that it was sexual, just that we're not one of that batch.

Susan: What was the relationship, if any, between thinking of yourself as a lesbian and being sexual?

Hazel: [Long pause.] Once you know that you are a lesbian, then being sexual becomes a real choice you need to make. It becomes one of the potentials.

Susan: Did it make it more likely you were going to become sexual with Nancy?

Hazel: Oh yes!

Susan: Tell me how that happened.

Hazel: Well, she got more and more unhappy with her marriage, and my tension and fear about the whole thing made me sick. I had an asthma attack that was so severe I almost died. When I got out of the hospital, things had changed; a crisis like that puts everything in perspective. It had occurred to me that I was mortal, and that life felt really good. And the question of who touched what body parts seemed so small. I just couldn't take all that seriously, whether society was going to fret if I slept with her or not.

So we went off on a vacation together. I remember back rubs through and under our flannel shirts. And, "Well, it's kind of cold. Maybe we should move our sleeping bags together." I think what we actually did was probably not all that much, but I remember feeling wet for the first time. And being really spacey, a sort of spacey feeling. When this is so new, it doesn't take a whole lot of touching to be way off somewhere. It was all quite wonderful.

The touching was equal, mutual, and tentative. I was clearly a butch, that was obvious, and she saw herself as being a butch too. That was slightly confusing, but not very.

Susan: What did that mean to you, that you were a butch?

Hazel: I had grown up being a tomboy. And at that time — let me say in my defense, we're talking the early sixties here — being a tomboy meant being really scornful of a lot of stuff women were or were thought to be. I saw being a butch as being an independent, competent woman. I had no concept of femme as a real lesbian identity.

How I knew butch/femme was from Gold Medal books, a series of trash novels available in the fifties and sixties. In them the relationships tended to be pretty much butch/femme, and they all came out badly. Various people committed suicide or at least walked off unhappily into the distance. The femme member of the unit usually got married to somebody.

I thought then that butch/femme was about who flirted with whom in a bar, and that femmes were...I don't know what I thought they were. They were women being women according to how our culture saw feminine, and I didn't care for it.

Susan: Then what happened between Nancy and you?

Hazel: Once we became sexual, Nancy and I had a relationship where she was married, and for two years we carried on this affair. I had to figure out how to spend a lot of time sneaking around and not feel guilty. I think I accomplished that through humor and perspective, by seeing the situation as a soap opera.

By that time I was a college teacher, and so was her husband. I'd come in in the morning, teach my first class, he'd be downstairs in his office, and I'd grab my coat and go out to breakfast with his wife. Or he would go off to work, and she'd come over to my apartment in the mornings. I knew her husband, I liked him, he liked me, and we hated each other's guts. I also knew she wasn't sexual with him.

Susan: She wasn't sexual with him?

Hazel: No. He was a gay man, but did we know it? No-o-o.

Susan: Once you and Nancy became sexual, did it feel like it changed the nature of your relationship?

Hazel: No, it didn't. It's not as if we had been friends first and then became sexual. It's like we had been in love for a long time first. Being sexual was just fulfilling that side of it. The being sexual was really nice, though, a kind of "coming home" feeling for me.

Susan: What do you think that "coming home" feeling is?

Hazel: Sex can be a time when I totally slow down and am in the present moment, a time when my body and spirit are in the same place. Also, when you're a lesbian in a culture that never wanted you to have your life anyway, sex is a very reassuring, a very affirming way of being yourself, no matter what, no matter how hard it was to get here. It's being who I was intended to be.

Susan: Is being sexual with women important to defining yourself as a lesbian?

Hazel: It is for me, but I don't know that that's the case for everybody. But for me if I'm not being sexual, I feel like I'm in the closet again. And I hate that! Because being in the closet is not a thing I want in my life. I did that. No more, no. I don't feel like a real lesbian if I'm not allowing myself to have my sexual feelings and to be sexual.

If I went through some time without being sexual, that would not change my identity. But I would try very hard not to have that happen. I think it's sad how many obstacles a lot of lesbians and a lot of women have to being sexual. Of course it's not an easy thing to figure out, 'cause it's not just whether you jump into bed with somebody or not. It's how to be who you really are.

Hazel and Nancy's relationship continued for seven years, ending in 1969 when Hazel was twenty-eight. Hazel moved on to other women, first in a series of one- to three-year serially semimonogamous relationships.

Susan: Can you characterize a pattern for yourself in those early years?
Hazel: Usually there was one person who was crucially important to me, but I might very well be sexual with somebody else at the same time. I was always clear where my loyalties were, that this is my main relationship here. I was pretty open about it, I wasn't being sneaky.
Susan: So you could do that emotionally, without ... ?
Hazel: I could do that emotionally. Even back when I was with Nancy I fell in lust with this neat woman, who was very athletic and very femme. We had a nice relationship for some months, including being sexual, but were clear that our primary loyalties were with our original partners. Both of our relationships did break up over it, nor did she and I stay together, but at the time, how did we know how to do anything else?

Hazel continued her semimonogamous pattern for seven years, and then in 1976, after the breakup of a particularly painful one-and-a-half-year relationship, she began a four-year period of noncommitted experimentation.

Hazel: These were brief alliances, friendships that included sex for a while. We tried not to be tacky or exploitative with each other. There'd be this attraction, "Let's act on it."

One time I remember we were out on a farm, way back in the cornfields — cornfields can be incredibly private — and we were making love out there. There were a bunch of dogs, mine and various other people's, who picked up all this sexual energy and were bouncing around being giddy. The sun was shining, and it was also raining, crazy raindrops coming down. It felt totally earthy and fun.

Another time a woman said, "Will you walk me home? I'm afraid." If somebody gives me a line like Will you walk me home? I feel like I'm turning the pages of a novel; I just have to see what happens. Unfortunately, once we got there, she had to pretend to be drunk to start being sexy.

Then there was a woman who didn't speak any English. Our only common language was French, mine was pretty rusty, and hers was heavily accented Swiss-German. We couldn't have all those endless talks that lesbians do, like spending until six in the morning discussing, Are we going to get into this or not? when it's a foregone conclusion. So we spent a lot of time shrugging and grinning and laughing. It was real clear we were fantasy figures to each other. She seemed to see me as this young American butch, therefore very free. And, since she was quite a bit older and had steel gray hair, I saw her as worldly and European. It was just a stitch.

Susan: Do you find yourself being the initiator in relationships?

Hazel: I'm likely to do a fair amount of the actual

pursuing and clarifying, but what really happens is somebody comes along who is attracted to me. They're putting out that kind of energy, which is one of the things I find very erotic, and I respond to it.

Also, when I'm being the initiator, or when we're playing out butch/femme dynamics, that's very often when I experience female ejaculation. I'll be lying on top of someone — usually someone I've been with for a while so there's more feeling in the connection — and I have this very intense orgasm.

Susan: Can you describe what it feels like?

Hazel: [Long pause.] It's just this force-of-nature kind of feeling. It's turning myself over to whatever this force of sex is that runs us. It feels . . . I love the feeling! It's a great sense of release.

And sometimes I'm lucky enough to be with somebody who thinks this is absolutely wonderful. So, when I go off to see her, I just bring my towels along. Why don't people make sexier towels?

Susan: I know you were looking for principles to guide your sexual behavior. What were some that you came up with?

Hazel: Well, one we've talked about, that women don't do sex in a casual way. Another is not always workable, but it's good in principle, which is not to get involved with anyone who doesn't feel good about themselves. It's not that sex can't be a huge consolation, but if people have a big hole they're trying to fill up, it's not a good place to start.

Also, I didn't want to have a pattern I was supposed to fit into, like when somebody's casting around for a life companion, with the roses in the yard and the picket fence and a dog and cat, and they're trying you out for the part.

And I tried to avoid having a relationship be an entity in itself. With one woman it seemed like our relationship was this really bratty little kid that sat between us, each of us holding its hand. It felt weird. I want relating to be a verb that describes how we are and what happens with us together, not a noun that you have to try to live up to.

Without quite intending it, Hazel's years of brief relationships gradually came to an end. Sixteen years ago, when she was thirty-eight, she began a long-term relationship with Fran. The two are still together.

Hazel: We met when we were taking a workshop together. I remember looking at her and thinking, Now who is this very interesting person? We started kind of flirting slowly, and going out and doing things together. She felt that she was a lesbian, but she had not yet been in a lesbian relationship. So it was slow developing, but at our second meeting I had this little click of recognition.

Susan: Do you think of that "click" as falling in love?

Hazel: No, though I bet some people do. What it means to me is that somebody has come into my life who is going to be important to me. It means I'm going to take some risks here, that there's a potential for intimacy. I think, Well, now we're gonna turn down that trail and see what happens.

It took three or four months until I got Fran in bed.

Now at the time I was still in a relationship with a woman named Dorothy; it had lasted about a year. And at first it was amazing to have two people, Fran and Dorothy, both of whom I cared about very much and was serious about and was being sexual with. I felt an incredible sense of joy and freedom — I can still remember almost a physical rush of energy — because there was a big taboo I had broken, the taboo that you can't have more than one relationship at a time.

You're breaking this taboo on one level when you're seeing somebody pretty regularly, but also dating and seeing other people. But that's not very profoundly breaking it. When you have two people, both of whom you care about, and both of whom you're having a serious relationship with, that was clearly a new thing for me. It was very freeing. It felt to me like the kind of step you take in becoming a lesbian in the first place, and saying, I like it, I'm happy about this, I'm proud. It was a coming out kind of feeling.

But it was a bit of a logistics problem and a tact problem, and then it got complicated because neither one of them was happy with it.

I stopped being able to do it when I found I had no time for me. I'm not that much of an extrovert, and there just was not time and energy to go around. So in practical terms, it does not work to have two relationships. We're just not constructed this way, and time is too short.

Eventually Dorothy and I broke up, though we have remained friends. Fran and I didn't move in together for four years; we were kind of a joke among our friends. But if you're two relatively shy and pretty autonomous people, you don't want to rush things.

We were active sexually at the beginning in a matter-of-fact way, like of course that's what we'd be doing with the kind of energy we have between us. But shortly after that it began to worry me that we weren't more sexual. If we weren't being sexual once a week or once every two weeks, I would feel an absence, and I'd be trying to pursue or initiate it, and nothing was happening. I'd try to just quietly stir things up, assuming some attraction should be there, and it wouldn't be, and it would be too embarrassing to try to talk about it, or if I would try to talk about it, then she wouldn't.

So it went on like this for a while, and then I got in a fling. Fran and I had talked about monogamy, we'd said how we were getting serious, and we were going to be together a long time, and it was pretty unlikely we'd go through all of life and neither one of us ever be sexual with anybody else. So what would be the least damaging ways that that would happen? We tried to discuss it theoretically, never referring to an actual situation.

We decided if it came out of positive feelings rather than feelings of lacking or bitterness or resentfulness, that would be one good thing. And it could be quite glorious, but it'd have to be of short duration. And somebody who was elsewhere, so it didn't infringe on our life together.

My fling really met all those conditions. It happened away from Milwaukee, at a conference, and so on. And Fran handled it pretty well. But then I got reinvolved with the same woman, and was deceptive with Fran, and that had a whole different feeling. I knew right away that what didn't make this okay was that I was angry with Fran. And having been sexual with this woman, I realized there was a piece of myself that was missing.

It's true that Fran and I weren't being sexual nearly as often as I wanted, but mostly I felt that her energy wasn't in it. I couldn't flirt with her and get any feedback, any uptake. And she became ticklish, and where she was ticklish grew, just like a rash spreading.

For a while it was really hard, because our relationship was very good, but we had horrible fights about sex. Now I had known that she had been sexually abused by her father, but she was not discussing it in any way, so it didn't feel okay for me to bring it up. Then memories of incest began cropping up spontaneously, and Fran knew she had to deal with it.

We had some worse fights along the way, but it's become better because I can stop taking it personally and feeling so mystified. I know the fact that she does not feel sexual is not a relationship issue, it's an abuse issue. What's true is that when we became really close and intimate in other ways, then it became impossible for her to be intimate and sexual.

Susan: Have you found ways to be intimate that are not sexual?

Hazel: The fact that Fran and I really talk about what's going on — it's not the same cozy intimacy of sex, and it's not even intimacy you like sometimes — but it's definitely intimacy and very real. We've been through some pretty hellish times along the way working all this stuff out.

Then about three years ago — Fran and I had been together twelve years by this time — I had a very intense dream. There was a party in the living room of some lesbian friends from my past, and I was being flirtatious in a generic way. When I woke up I was lying there not wanting to drop the heavy sexual feeling of the dream. And suddenly I realized I could not remember what my own living room was like, I could not think what my house looked like now. And a minute later I thought, yeah, "living room," in a sense I don't have it. There's something I need to think about here that has to do with a piece of myself that I've lost.

Just before this dream I'd had a phone conversation with a woman I knew from my past. Later we met again, and she was really attracted to me. I was picking up on the energy and becoming quite pleased and flattered and nervous. We didn't actually get sexual until some months later, because I knew this was going to be a big thing if we did.

Jessica and I have been lovers now for over two years. She is also in a committed relationship — a fifteen- or sixteen-year relationship — and we both know what is missing in our long-term relationships. But we are loyal to them, and we intend to stay with them.

I've been scrupulously honest with Fran about this. I don't want to have fights about it. I want us to be working on our own relationship so that things progress. I know she still really hates the idea of my being lovers with Jessica, but much of the time her attitude is very good humored. She can even sometimes say, "It's been good for you."

Susan: What about it has been good for you?

Hazel: I'm more happy and more self-confident. I no longer feel like another victim of Fran's incestuous family. There's some part of me that's alive if I'm being sexual, and I like that part of me a lot; I'm on good terms with it.

Jessica's and my relationship is based on a very solid friendship, and it's based on a lot of lust. There's a wonderful kind of humor in dealing with adolescent energy when you're solidly in your fifties. We can be playful in ways I would not have expected. Like she has some black lace number . . . she can be so bold sometimes. And she's always been very attracted to butch women, but was afraid to explore that. So it feels quite experimental. And the sexual charge stays there because we are playing within limits; we don't get to see each other that much, so why waste time talking!

Jessica and I don't even know what terms to use for ourselves. We're lovers. But it's not an affair, god knows. It's an arrangement for dealing with life as it really is. I think there's a tradition for this, but I don't think it's on this continent.

I think the form that sex takes between two people comes out of that particular relationship; it does not mean following rules. Being primary with one woman and sexual with another woman feels like figuring out what hand you've been dealt and doing the best you can with it. In being lovers with Jessica I'm finding a side of myself that I hadn't even known. But that's not all of me.

There's a lot of emotional intensity between Fran and me, and it's easy for me to imagine that I could find a sexual way to tap into that. But that doesn't mean that she would. I couldn't tell you what I think the real bond is with Fran and me right now, but it's there. There's some way we're really suited to each other. But right now we're simply trying not to have sex be a difficult thing between us.

Saudia

"The last man I was with was nice. I
think for my last try at 'Is this really
what I want?' it was good. But the sex
lacked ... the sex lacked breasts."

My first partner was a nun in another order. We met
at a Black Sisters conference. She asked, "Do you want to
bunk with me?" and I said, "Fine." She said, "Okay, I'll
get two beds." So the first night I slept in my bed and I
was good. The second night I looked at her and said, "Can
I sleep with you tonight?" And I meant sleep. She said,
"Sure."

We were talking, and she kissed me and ... [Saudia

claps her hands] then she was on top of me. It was okay because I still didn't put anything together. Then she started touching me, and I didn't know what that meant. I freaked completely out. I said, "Women don't do this." And she said, "Oh ho, yes they do." And I said, "Are you sure?" And she said, "Well, if you'd be still you'd find out."

Saudia is a forty-nine-year-old African-American woman, of average height, a bit heavier and a bit more gray than she'd like to be. We talked in her colorful and crowded studio apartment in downtown Albuquerque, squeezed in among the double bed, a desk overflowing with papers, a kitchen alcove heaped with dishes, a tropical-fish tank, and the wood-and-paper scale-model airplane she had built, a Fokker Triplane, wingspan nearly four feet. Her Yorkshire terrier, Warrior, hovered near us, watching intently and twitching protectively.

Saudia wore a red, yellow, and orange T-shirt, tie-dyed in a circular sun pattern, but her cheerful clothes were in contrast to the story she had to tell. Life has often felt frightening to Saudia, and her connections to her own body have not always been comprehensible or satisfying. She is blessed with a sense of humor, but talking about sex does not come easily. At the beginning of the interview Saudia cautioned me, "I told one of my friends I'm doing this and she says, 'You can't even talk to *me* about sex.'" I assured Saudia it can be easier with a stranger. She remained skeptical.

Susan: When did you first learn about sex?
Saudia: When I was young I didn't know what sex was; I was kind of removed from my body. My parents both worked, which meant that my brother and I had to

take care of each other when we got home from school. We weren't supposed to go outside or even open the door.

Nonetheless, when I was nine I got involved with this little boy next door. He was about two years older and knew everything; I knew nothing.

Susan: What did he want to do?

Saudia: He wanted to do the adult thing.

Susan: Was it exciting at all, or not?

Saudia: The exciting part was being out of the house. I just felt so good being out. "See," I said to myself, "nothing bad happened to me." But a neighbor turned us in. I got in trouble; it was very upsetting, very frightening. It took me a very long time to tell my mother what happened between me and the boy, and I never told my father.

I thought of that situation every day of my life until after I left the convent, over twenty years later. I thought about how bad I was, and how unforgiven I was.

Susan: By your parents?

Saudia: By God. The Catholic Church and my mother told me that women were stronger than men, and that men would follow our lead. So, if anything happened, it would definitely be my fault.

Susan: Did she ever try to explain anything about sex to you?

Saudia: Well, right after the experience with the neighbor boy I started my first period, and she explained that. That's when I got really concerned, because I asked, "How many times do you have to do this to get a baby?" And she said, "Once," and disappeared.

As I grew up I felt very ill at ease with boys. I loved to dance, but was very afraid. In high school a friend of my father's made overtures to me, and I became very frightened. I'm still more nervous than complimented when black men pay attention to me.

I found it much more comforting to be around girls.

And at eighteen, after high school graduation, I joined the convent. My mother, who pretty much ruled our house, was very proud of me; I could do no wrong, I was walking on water. I know now that I entered the convent because I was in great fear of not understanding what was happening.

Susan: About sex, or about life in general?

Saudia: Life in general. Just everything. I was very afraid and knew I couldn't do it by myself. So when I entered I knew I was going to be protected.

Susan: Were you devout as well?

Saudia: Yes. The whole family was. When we didn't have a car we would walk to church, even though it was a long way. And we didn't have a lot of money, but we always gave to the church.

Susan: Were you a sexual person in the convent?

Saudia: No! No! No! [Then she laughs and says, "I'm only teasing you."] Seriously, no. I never thought of myself as a sexual person. Once when I was in the convent in Knoxville one of the nuns came on to me, but I didn't know that that's what it was, so it didn't make me feel uncomfortable in the slightest. I just thought maybe they did things differently in the South.

Susan: Can you tell me what happened between you and her?

Saudia: One time we were in this old, old house, with a spiral staircase and all. They said it had been used as part of the underground railroad. We were in one of the rooms, fixing hot chocolate for the other nuns. I turned around to do something, and she kissed me, her lips landing a bit off-center. I said, "Would you not do that?" And she said, "One of these days I'm gonna get it right on the lips."

Susan: How old were you?

Saudia: We were all in our young to mid-twenties.

I made my final vows, and then moved around the country teaching. I have some pictures from those days.

Saudia rummages around in her desk and emerges with several pictures of herself and other Catholic women. In one she is dressed in her full nun's habit, and looks out at the camera, fresh faced and very sweet looking. "I was nineteen or twenty in this picture and had just completed my postulant year, my first," she explains. She hands me another picture. "And here we all are at the Black Sisters conference, where I met my first lover." A half dozen young, dark-skinned women in black habits have posed on the steps of a church. They stand tall, close to each other but not quite touching, smiling proudly at the camera.

Saudia: I know that when I fell in love with my first lover, I fell in love with the fact that I could be loved, that I could be cared for as an individual, because I hadn't had that. When I see her walking in my memory, I'd swear she is not walking on the ground. She was very intelligent, very self-assured. And yet she singled me out and cared for me.

Susan: You told me about stopping her from making love to you the first time you were in bed together. What happened next?

Saudia: Well, we lived in different cities. So the next time we were together, maybe six months later, we went to one of the convent rooms that wasn't being used. She had pants on, and I had a skirt on, and it was off before I got in the room. My underwear went flying, she was talking to me, and kissing me, and we lay down on the bed and made love. She kissed my neck and . . . oh God . . . she kissed my breasts . . . I'm very naked by now. And I think she still had her bra on, I remember helping her off with that. She had large breasts. She also had very small hands.

She had a habit of grabbing both my breasts and she'd smile. I liked seeing her pleasure.

Susan: Did you make love back to her?

Saudia: A little. I felt like a kindergartner, but she never made me feel ill at ease. When we were separated, she would make love to me over the phone. It was great. She would be talking about something else entirely, like, "I was trying to catch the bus," and then, "I saw us making love and you were coming." It would just go right through me. I would feel like she was right there touching me.

She would talk about the process: That I was coming over that night, and she would be getting things ready. She would meet me with a kiss, and both of us would be kissing and taking our clothes off at the same time. She would have gotten new sheets, and she'd describe the sheets and what the bed looked like. Then we'd be in bed, and she'd be on top of me, and out of nowhere comes this cucumber. In those days we were too poor to have any sex toys, so we mostly used things like cucumbers, you know. She would describe tracing it down the length of my body . . . I can't say any more.

Susan: You're doing wonderfully. [We both laugh.]

Could you have an orgasm when she was talking to you on the phone?

Saudia: Yes. Just from her words. I think especially the last year we were separated, it kept me alive. She had a lot to give.

One time, we were making love and she had come, and I had come really, really hard. I usually tighten up in a fetal position afterward. She said, "I've got a surprise for you." She jumped out of bed, ran to the icebox, came back and said, "Relax, relax." She inserted an ice cube in my vagina. It was phenomenal. I was on complete fire and all of a sudden: Cold! It was amazing, like an explosion inside me.

At that time I was just enjoying sex so much, and

getting more and more physically involved with my life, and being okay with that. It was really good.

But I don't know what love is anymore. When I think back, I was with her for nine years, and I knew I was not in love within two years of being with her. But I stayed because as long as she was happy, I was happy. But later she started spending less time with me, and drinking. Then she would come upstairs in the middle of the night and wake me up for sex. During the day, though, she never talked to me. Eventually I packed up and left. But I think losing her was like, No one will ever love me again. That was ten years ago. My fear now, that I have to keep down, is that I'm going to die alone, you know.

The whole time I was with her, though, I was not gay. I was just with her. Since I left, I have chosen to be a lesbian. My counselor says I'm bisexual. And I said, "Well, I don't really understand men, and they do scare me, and I want to be with someone." So I have chosen to have my world dominated by women.

Susan: Some people argue that being a lesbian or being gay is genetic. Does it feel like a choice to you?

Saudia: Yeah, it does to me. Gays are all over the place, different shapes and sizes and colors. So, to say we all choose, or we're all genetic, is too simple.

Did you hear that they're looking at tomboys now, in part to track lesbianism? Who the fuck cares! They are good healthy kids, running around, sticking their tongues out, playing with this, playing with that; they're happy girls. Leave them alone. No, I don't believe that it's in our genes.

Susan: Since you broke up with your nun partner ten years ago, what have you been doing with your romantic and sexual life?

Saudia: I have gone out with women and one man. Let's get the man thing over with first. He was a guy I met at a bar. We met and did a lot of different things, and made love five times. I know because I had a box of six rubbers. It was nice. He was very gentle. He was a jerk, but I think for my last try at, Is this really what I want? it was good. I wasn't afraid of him at all.

But he didn't have any breasts! [Laughter.] I kept reaching for them! The experience in total was good, I think, but the sex lacked ... the sex lacked breasts. The smells were different. Men and women are funky, but male funky is not attractive to me. And when we kissed, he had stubble.

But if I had to do it, I'm glad I did it with him because he had some respect for me.

The women I've been with ... one in particular, we would just make love all night long, go to sleep, wake up, and continue. It was just phenomenal. When one of us tried anything new we didn't just do it, we said, "Is this okay?" or "Would you mind if I tried ... ?" or "I want to see if you like this." It was nice to see her face; she was very into what she was doing, but also very pleased.

I really miss her, because I know that at least we had the sex part down right. It's the other part, you know, the personality stuff we didn't really have.

Susan: What's one of your favorite things to do sexually?

Saudia: I love kissing. I *love* kissing. And when I have a new lover there's a way I try to get familiar with the body and the person; I just kiss everything. I call it "blessing the body."

The other thing I like — I haven't done it in so long, I don't know if I can do it again — is the two-headed dildo. I like that! We have this problem, women do, that if you're taking care of business orally, you're out of focus (my age talking here), you can't touch. A two-headed dildo makes it possible to feel as much of the body as you can.

Susan: So you can do vaginal orgasms?

Saudia: I don't understand.

Susan: There's a running debate about whether or not women have vaginal orgasms or whether they even exist.

Saudia: [Much laughter.] Just touch my nose and I can come! Seriously, I come both ways, vaginal or clitoris.

Susan: Do you have a preference?

Saudia: [Long pause.] Yes I do. The vaginal. My last partner — we were together two years and two months — I was only the second person she was with. After a while I could not come, but when we started talking about toys and stuff, her comment was, "I only want things that are natural."

Susan: The whole lesbian thing's unnatural according to some.

Saudia: I thought so, and that's what I said: Two women together, give me a break. It was incredible. But she would not do any kind of toys. I have a vibrator, but she said, "No vibrators." Okay, then I have a dildo. "No." Then she would get tired using her fingers. And she could come easily with just external stuff, no penetration. It seemed selfish.

So it was very hard for me. I take antidepressant medication, and it has side effects, you know. Affects your sex response. When I come, I come very powerfully. But when I don't come, I don't come.

Susan: So that was the end of your sexual relationship?

Saudia: Yeah. I liked her. But I decided I don't want to live my life like that, if she wasn't going to try to make me happy.

Susan: What do you do about protecting yourself from AIDS and other sexually transmitted diseases?

Saudia: When I feel like I'm going to have sex with someone I ask that the person get a test. I talk about it right up front with whoever before anything happens. And I keep up with tests myself. I thought I would be strong enough to say, If you're not going to have the test, then we won't do anything. But this last person wouldn't go get a test. And I said okay anyway.

Susan: Do you use dental dams, Saran Wrap, that kind of thing?

Saudia: Before this last person I just did the test and thought that was enough. But now I know it's not. I have a safer-sex kit and intend to use it.

But I don't know how to date. I don't know how to attract. I'm forty-nine years old, thirteen years in the convent, nine years with just one woman, and I'm supposed to know what I'm doing? It's phenomenally difficult.

Susan: What's your sexual life like now?

Saudia: I have my vibrator; we became acquainted again.

And I have a crush on a woman. In talking to her I know she's sensual. I like someone who touches. Who enjoys feeling good. I'm a tactile person. I want to be held.

She's rather butch, another black woman. In this town, black women are very scarce. Black lesbians.

Susan: You're not interested in being with a Caucasian woman or Asian or other varieties?

Saudia: Anything that stands still.

Susan: Pardon me?

Saudia: Anything that stands still. [Much laughter between us.] No, seriously. The last person I was with was white. I've been with a Latina. No. I don't do race stuff; I try to keep racism out of me. A woman is a woman, you know.

Crystal

"My fist is my best toy."

I come from a very loving family; my father adored my mother, held her in high esteem. And I'm the oldest of three girls, yet my father did not want a son. I think his attitude toward women has a great deal to do with why I'm the type of butch woman I am.

I'm an old-school butch woman, not just because I'm older, but because I hold a lot of the butch traditions very near and dear to my heart. I have such an appreciation for women, and for me that appreciation can turn into action. Where another butch might say to a woman "You look very nice," I will act on that fact, by kissing her hand or her neck or whatever else I feel like and can get away with.

Crystal and I are sitting at a small table in a shabbily trendy cafe in Dallas. Though nestled in an alcove, we are close to the front door, surrounded by windows, easily visible from the street. Though the content of our talk is intensely personal, Crystal herself has chosen this exposed meeting place.

She is a handsome forty-seven-year-old woman, with bright, dark eyes and short dark hair shot with much gray. She is dressed in a black shirt, ironed and buttoned to the neck, jeans pressed and accented with a black studded belt, polished black boots, and black wire-framed glasses, an austere, formal dress, a costume. Her manner is friendly — she responds openly and at length to my many questions — but her energy is, at the same time, completely self-contained. She leans back in her chair, her hands relaxed in her lap, only occasionally sitting forward to emphasize some intense point. She speaks with authority, but her eyes are warm.

Crystal: I am one of the very few women I know who does not come from an abused family. I was raised in the country, around horses and stuff, so as I sit here today with you in boots and jeans, not a whole lot has changed. I was a tomboy, but I never wanted to be a boy. I am not a male-identified butch as much as I look like I could be, because I am so happy and proud to be who I am. I am so strong in who I am, and that is in being a woman, that I see absolutely no reason to want to be anything else. But then, to me boys never had it over me because I was a girl; I could still do all the boy things. If I wanted the model gas station for Christmas, that's what I got. I didn't have to have the dolls.

Susan: So your parents didn't fight with you about what kind of little girl you were going to be.

Crystal: No! No! No! I was always supported for the type of girl that I was. Which allowed me to go ahead and end up being not just a tomboy, but a butch lesbian.

I feel that butches are a separate gender; they just don't have a name for us. We're not transsexuals. We're not transgender. We're not males. We're not females. We're something in the middle. I consider myself a separate gender that has qualities of both.

Susan: Does it mean you're androgynous?

Crystal: Oh god no! Are you kidding? Look at me. This is not androgynous staring at you. Every day that I leave my house I am a statement walking down the street: I'm a dyke.

Susan: Tell me about the tradition of being butch.

Crystal: When I was nineteen and coming out as a lesbian, I had mentors. The year was 1966, and I remember being told that I would either have to be butch or femme. That was the way it was. Well, I was sitting there in jeans and a shirt and boots and short hair. We all laughed because it was quite obvious what I was going to be.

So I had older butch women talk to me, teach me. They showed me how to bind my breasts 'cause that was the thing that we did. I looked like a little Italian boy. A lot of it for them was trying to pass as men. But for me, it was never my intention to really pass. I was just finding out my own sexuality within myself.

I learned those old traditions that go along with being butch, like how you treat the women that you date. They are treated like ladies; you always open the door and you pay the bill and, to protect them, you walk on the street side of the sidewalk. Though nowadays everything is so bizarre I wonder where in the hell is the safest place to put them.

So I learned the concern, the protectiveness. And I learned the appreciation. I have a huge amount of appreciation for feminine women who I feel walk the same path I do. I think their struggle is the same, even though it is different in that they can pass if they choose. So, if I am dating someone who's extremely feminine, I appreciate the time she has taken to present herself, to get herself ready. She may be out on the street and get whistled at by men, or may get comments made when she walks down the street with me. But she's willing to risk it, mirroring who I am, you know.

I also learned as a butch always to be aggressive. Butches never took their pants off. Packing — you know, wearing and using dildos — was not really talked about at the time except in quiet little corners. Now everybody talks about it, at least in the S/M community; it's no big deal. I guess in the vanilla community it's still kind of a touchy issue. They just don't want to admit that a dildo might feel good, and it's okay. I say that there's really no heavy political implications here, girls; we can just have a good time with it. It's an appendage. It's another toy to fuck my girlfriend with, thank you very much. I put it on, it doesn't mean I want to be a man. For me, anyway. For others I know that they do.

So I learned about being aggressive, but also about being tender, making sure that you didn't rush, that you satisfied the woman. One of my butch mentors was fifty years old when I was nineteen. The others were in their late twenties. So I had input from different generations. They got their little hands on me and made different influences.

When they took me to a lesbian bar, that was it for me. I drank like a fish and got very bold, picking women up that I didn't know, convincing them to go home with me and making love to them, and them not knowing this was maybe my first, second, or third time I'd done this type of thing. I had no idea what I was doing, but it seemed to work okay 'cause there were no complaints. I was nineteen. Everything happened when I was nineteen; it was a great year.

And then I progressed from there. It was fun.

Susan: Can you remember what you'd say when you approached them?

Crystal: Oh god no! I can hardly come up with anything now [we're laughing], let alone remember what I said so long ago. Hopefully, I've improved. I don't know, but I would hope so.

Susan: So when you say you didn't take your pants off when you had sex with a woman, does that mean your partners didn't make love to you?

Crystal: Right. That went on until I was in my mid-twenties, until I was finally with a woman who said to me, "Either I make love to you and then you can make love to me, or you can go home now." So I thought, Hmmm, what do I want to do about that? Then I said, "Okay fine!" And it went from there.

Susan: So how did it feel to let her make love to you?

Crystal: I don't recall it feeling weird or anything of the sort. But to this day I am more comfortable with my pants on until I really, really know somebody and trust them. I think a lot of butch women have vulnerability issues, and that's one of them. You take your pants off, you're extremely vulnerable. That's it: You're to the max.

I think that's one thing with butches, I think we have trouble being vulnerable. Femmes are emotionally very strong. Butches are little mushes inside, and in order to take care of that we build these huge walls, and we only let in those women that we really trust.

Susan: When you were young, what was the preferred mode for having sex: oral sex or hands or dildos or what?

Crystal: Well, I know what my friends and I talked about, but I don't know what was done. Oral sex was talked about a lot, and I think we probably did it a hell of a lot more then than we do now. And that's because of AIDS. I don't know what the vanilla community is doing out there, but I know the S/M dykes are either not doing oral sex or they're doing it with a barrier. Well, with a barrier, that's not the same thing.

Oral sex was fun, that was a good time. But now, unless you are in a monogamous relationship, and you've been there for a very long time, and you've both been tested, and you both are safe... if all those things aren't true, what are you going to do? You don't do oral sex very often.

But anyway, back then oral sex was talked about a lot, more so than I think anything else.

Susan: And did you do that yourself?

Crystal: Oh sure. That was fun, that was a good time.

Susan: And what else did you do?

Crystal: I did everything I could.

I had sought out Crystal because she was a central figure in the S/M community in Dallas, someone experienced, knowledgeable, and articulate about the attitudes and activities that make up this significant sexual subculture in the lesbian community.

Susan: When did the S/M thing become an important part of your sex life?

Crystal: It's always been there. I was very fortunate that, for two and a half years, from the time I was nineteen until twenty-two, I had an older woman as my lover who was kinkier than shit. She was the one who introduced me to really bizarre sex. That ranged anywhere from picking up a straight man and bringing him home, to being fucked with a foam-covered Coke bottle. Being tied up . . . it ran the gamut. And I just thought it was great fun. You know, certain people make you blossom.

I didn't know what it was; there were no names for it at the time. We didn't talk about it, like we do now, we just did it.

I'm trying to think if I've had any long-term relationships where we didn't do something in the realm of S/M, but we always have. I was with a woman for seven and a half years, from age twenty-four 'til thirty or so. We had mirrors above the bed, we had chains on the bed, we did bizarre stuff. Our friends thought we were weird.

But things have changed so drastically in the last ten years around S/M. It's not underground any more. Now you can take classes and find out how to do things correctly, which I'm all in favor of. We have communities and a history. There's ritual involved, and spirituality. We do a lot of role playing, a lot of fantasy play, which is just outrageous. It's dominance and submission. It's power exchange. I mean, here you are as adults, you get to do what you want to do.

Susan: How do you and another woman figure out what you're going to do together?

Crystal: You negotiate it. You talk about it beforehand. You approach someone and you say, "I would like to play with you." Meaning act out some fantasy. "And this is what I would like. How do you feel about it?" "Play" within our community means just that, playing. Because that's what it is. It's fun.

If I have a fantasy that I want to be a cop on the

street and arrest somebody and take 'em home and fuck 'em, I get to do that. I negotiate it with my partner or whomever. I say, "This is what I'd like. I'd like you to be standing in front of XY&Z, and I'm gonna come along and put you up against the wall. I'm gonna handcuff you and take you off..." and away we go. Well, what a great fantasy that is.

It's endless. Wherever your imagination takes you is where you get to go. And we talk about our fantasies. "This is what I want, this is what I think I would like to see happen. Do you think you can work this out with me?" Yes, it's hard to talk, it is for us too. But if we're going to get what we want, we can get up the courage to ask.

We are more willing to explore any sexual angle that we can get, probably more so than most. In fact we have a lot of different people who do a lot of gender fucking in our community.

Susan: What's gender fucking?

Crystal: We have people who are transgender, who are making physical sexual changes. We have women who want to pass as men. We have "daddies" that are women. We have young butch women who are calling themselves boys. It's hard to keep up with sometimes, even for someone who's in the community. What unites us is that we're so open to exploring all parts of who we are sexually.

Susan: Can you tell me what it is about an S/M situation that is spiritual?

Crystal: We have rituals with each other that are an honoring of the person, a gift. Here's an example: I have given my partner a permanent piercing on her labia. It was part of our commitment to each other. And here's another example: I have a scarification on my arm. A woman with whom I had a relationship drew a rose on my arm and then literally cut it with a scalpel. Her gift to me was the cutting. She is the only woman I have ever been the bottom for. I was giving over to her my power and my control, and in doing so, that was the ultimate trust. And she treated my trust very, very well. That was a tremendously powerful ritual.

She lived in another state, and at the end of the times we would spend together, when one of us would have to fly away, she would recut the rose. So when she would leave . . . see, I'll even get choked up telling you about it [Crystal is blinking back tears] . . . the rose would always be with me, which it is to this day.

We are also a community that believes we are a family, so we take care of our family. We just lost one of our members not too long ago, and there were benefits held, people organizing to help the family pay for the funeral expenses.

And I am talking here, not about the family of the lesbian community, but about the family of the leather women's community. A lot of the lesbian community still doesn't like us. They think we're really bad people, and we're not.

Susan: Why do you think the larger lesbian community objects to S/M?

Crystal: Because they can't separate S/M from abuse. They think we're abusers. And they think those who are bottoming for us want to be abused. They themselves are so frightened, and have been abused so much themselves, that they can't conceive of how giving someone else control over you can be a wonderful place to be. They can't conceive that S/M has to do with power and trust. They can't conceive of how pain can be enjoyable. No matter what you say, no matter how you try and explain it, they don't get that. So how can they possibly understand? And most of them aren't willing to take the time to find out more either.

But we're just like they are. We just get to play a lot better than they do. Because they don't talk about their sex lives. We sit down and say, "I loved the way you fisted me. Now I want you to do it again . . . and I want you to do it again." Or, "I want you to roll me over and fuck my ass." I mean, we don't have a problem being really honest with each other and asking for what we want.

Susan: How is it that pain can be enjoyable?

Crystal: Well, it's real different when you want something and you ask for it than when you don't. Like a flogging can be a great massage if it is done correctly. You warm up the woman who's receiving the flogging very gently, so the whip is hardly touching her at all, and then it builds. What happens is the whip becomes an extension of the person who wields it. So she's not only feeling pain, but she knows the whip and the pain are an extension of who I am.

Then, as you build, after a while it is no longer painful. Endorphins eventually kick in, so she gets high. Once the endorphins start, her body makes chemical changes which change her perception of what she's feeling. And that's where it's very important to have a good, responsible, knowledgeable top, because she wants more — she's saying "More, more, harder, harder" — and a good top can judge, "No, I think you've had enough now; you need to take a rest."

Susan: What about alcohol and drugs?

Crystal: I don't recommend it. There are people who do, but I argue you should do this clearheaded. You're going to get high anyway, so why not enjoy the altered state you're going to get to. That's my train of thought.

Susan: And what about HIV/AIDS?

Crystal: I think of HIV/AIDS as being a serious danger.

Susan: What do you think is the most dangerous behavior?

Crystal: Thinking that it won't happen to me. I think that is our biggest risk. Because I think it's possible anally or orally or vaginally. It depends on the person. It depends on the circumstances. So why take the risk? Why do you

want to risk your life for a fuck, is what it really boils
down to.

Susan: What precautions do you take against HIV/AIDS
infection doing S/M stuff?

Crystal: It depends on the different things you're doing.
If you play blood sports, you wear gloves. If you fist, you
wear gloves. Any sexual thing, you always wear gloves. If
you're play-piercing, you make sure the needles are clean.

Susan: What else do you do in S/M play to ensure
everyone's safety?

Crystal: When you negotiate to play with somebody —
"play" meaning to enact a fantasy — you choose a safe
word, and the top person, the one who is dominant or in
control, honors that safe word. So, if something's going on
and the person on the bottom — the submissive one —
wants it to stop, they use their safe word. Everything
stops.

And you always ask if people have medical issues. For
instance, suppose they have a tendency to faint if they
stand up too long. Or have asthma, so they need their
inhaler close by. Or cannot be penetrated because of such
and such. Whatever we choose to do we want to be well
informed, so we can play within a safe realm.

We would also talk about what experience the person
has had, whether sexually or with S/M. And, of course,
What do you think you like? What do you think you don't
like? What are you willing to try? What are you not
willing to try? What have you already done? What have
you not done? Negotiations are just that: You negotiate it.

Susan: Could you tell me about some recent S/M
scenario you've done?

Crystal: This is an S/M scenario, but it's mostly based
on the butch/femme dynamic, which creates so much power
and so much energy. The woman I just broke up with —
we had been together four and a half years — had children,
so we didn't have very much time to play. One day her

daughter was going swimming with a friend and would be gone two hours. We wanted to play and have sex, but, my god, we had so little time. So we decided we would meet in thirty minutes in the kitchen. I would be a soldier, and she would be going on a blind date with this soldier.

So she went in a bedroom and put on some slinky sexy dress. Changing clothes took her out of being a mom and made her into the sexy woman, so the soldier and her could have this date. I went in another room, put on my uniform, and started going through performance anxiety, which you always have as the top because you're the one who's supposed to be so damn creative and come up with all this shit. So I'm walking downstairs, thinking, What am I gonna do, I don't have anything planned . . .

Well, the minute I saw her it didn't matter because we had the butch/femme dynamic going on. There she was, looking beautiful and luscious in this skin-tight dress that brought out . . . you know, all of a sudden I'm the lusting soldier. The next thing I know I've got her up on top of the counter in the kitchen, the dress hiked up, and we're gonna fuck right there. I fisted her first — my fist is my best toy — then I fucked her with a dildo. So that's part of S/M, because we were role playing and I got rough.

Susan: Could she relax enough to be fisted just like that, without any preparation?

Crystal: A lot of our preparation is looking at each other. I look at her and want to fuck her. She looks at me and wants to get fucked. You already know what you want.

And you've changed your clothes. If I hadn't changed my clothes and become the soldier, I wouldn't have been able to get it up, so to speak. By getting dressed and creating that character, it changes my whole attitude. It changes the look. It changes the way I walk. When I finally got back to her, she wasn't a "mom" any more, she was a "slut." It works real well.

Susan: It strikes me that the whole thing — I guess you could call it foreplay, before anybody has touched anybody — is highly intellectual.

Crystal: Of course. We talk. Then we dress and let our minds and imaginations work. It builds and it builds and it builds, and then you get back together and, boom!

Susan: Are you currently playing with anyone?

Crystal: There is a woman in her thirties, whom I've known for several years, who is extremely submissive. How do I know that? Because when she stands and talks to me, she puts her hands behind her back, which is a submissive stance. Its gets me going.

Susan: Meaning it's a turn-on?

Crystal: Definitely, because that's what I like. Now if someone is being submissive — if someone will more than likely end up on their knees in front of me — to me they're not only giving me their power and their trust, they're giving me a gift, and I'd better treat that gift with honor and respect.

So we were at my house. I was sitting in a chair, and I brought her over and put her down on the floor next to me, and took her hand and said, "I want you for my slave." She was very surprised. I said we would have to talk about it, and play a couple of times together, and take it slowly. I also said I was offering her the opportunity to be submissive in a very safe place, dominated by someone who would truly honor and praise her for being sub-missive. That I felt I could nurture her submissiveness, that I could let her be proud of it and teach her how to be proud of it.

I also said that she would have fun and get high, and there were probably things that I would do with her that she had not had done. We talked a little bit about playing with fire because that's my big thing; I play with fire. She wanted to know, would she be walking around with a chain and a collar lock twenty-four hours a day. I said I don't need to do that to somebody. I said when you step inside these doors, then you become mine. When you leave them, you're on your own.

I also told her I did not want to be sexual — that she would not fuck me and I would not fuck her — that this would strictly be S/M. I personally think that sex sometimes mucks up an S/M relationship. So I made it clear I didn't want to be involved intimately like that with somebody. I wanted to play, period.

She said, "Well what are you going to have me do? Come over and do your dishes?"

And I said, "No, I'll probably take you to the car races with me. I'll have you come over and sit by my feet and watch a video. You have a great back; I would love to flog your back. And there would be other things we'd do, but I don't know what they necessarily are right now."

Susan: It seems like such a relationship would be very intimate even if you weren't being sexual.

Crystal: Oh it is, it is. I had a slave for a year and a half, whom I was not sexual with, and it was the most intimate relationship I've ever had. She knew me better than anyone else ever has. And I trusted her completely.

Susan: Do you think of an S/M relationship as being inherently a sexual relationship or not?

Crystal: Of course, the hottest part is when you get it all — both sex and S/M — YIKES! Oh boy, see I squirm in my chair thinking about it, because it's so damn good; there's nothing that compares to it. And now I forgot your question, I'm sorry.

Susan: If the sex part isn't there in an S/M relationship, but it's still a turn-on . . . could you somehow straighten that out for me?

Crystal: Well, the sexual energy is there; I just don't act on it. I'm not physically attracted to that particular individual. For instance with the woman who may become my slave, I'm attracted to her submissiveness — it's just so nice, that sweet little grin she has as she puts her hands behind her back — but I'm not physically attracted to her.

I'm attracted to femmes. I'm not sexually attracted to butches, so I'm kind of limited in what gets me going. I'd be happier if there were more femmes around.

Susan: Would you play with butches?

Crystal: Oh yeah, I do. But I'm not sexually attracted to them. I can find them cute or adorable, but they can't get me going like femmes do. No way!

Of course there's something for me about having all the power and control in an S/M scene that is erotic. Even though it's an illusion, even though the other person can stop it, when you're doing the scene, it's very real. I mean I can have my hands around somebody's throat and be choking them, and if I'm not careful, that can be the last time they breathe. Well, that's very powerful, that's charged, and to me that can be very erotic and very sexual. The energy that you create with that person charges the room and charges you. It's an exchange of power that goes back and forth, back and forth, back and forth. If you step into a room where such a scene is going on, you will feel it in the air, and that air is very erotically charged.

If somebody's going to have that much trust in me, give me control so I can do with them as I will, that's heavy power. And power in itself can be very erotic.

Susan: Can you tell me about liking to play with fire?

Crystal: Number one, I make my own torches. I put alcohol — 70 percent isopropyl alcohol is what it is — carefully on someone's body, I light the torch and run it over their body, which means that they are on fire. Or I'll take cotton, put it in the alcohol, lay the person down and draw designs on them. Then I set those on fire.

Then my job, of course, as the top and being

responsible, is I only let it stay there so long and then put it out. Because otherwise you'll give them a burn, which is not my intent.

I'm real visual. I love the visual. It's great fun to see somebody's body on fire. And how I get high from doing that is, that if I don't control that flame, the person is in jeopardy. So there's high risk for them, and high risk for me.

Susan: What kind of safety measures do you take?

Crystal: A fire extinguisher is number one. And you have a wet towel so if you get too much flame on a person, you can put it out. I move flammable things out of the way. I keep the alcohol in a safe container that has a lid, which I close before lighting any fire. The person I play with can't wear anything that might ignite, like deodorant or cologne or hair spray. If they have long hair, they have to tie it up. And I use my arm as a shield. If I'm playing on somebody's back, for instance, I'll put my arm up by their neck so my arm feels the heat first. I also watch out for hot spots. If you keep setting a person's body on fire all the time, certain spots might get unusually sensitive and burn sooner than they would otherwise.

There are lots of safety issues to be aware of. I've been doing this for seven or eight years now, and have a lot of experience doing different things safely.

Susan: What else do you like to do?

Crystal: I go to a magic shop and get what they call flash paper. I lay somebody down, draw on them with alcohol, set them on fire, then stand above them with the flash paper and ignite it. If I put sparkle additive in it, it'll go POOF above them and these little sparkles will come down right over their body. It won't burn them if you get it up high enough, but they don't know that. So they have a fear factor going. And for me, it's control. Fire is a very intense element to control.

Susan: Have you always been interested in fire?

Crystal: Always. As a little kid I had a neighborhood friend who was a pyro. She would build me little fires. But she got real bad. She started doing buildings. Of course I started doing people!

As our interview drew to a close, Crystal had some final thoughts about the connections among butch/femme roles, sexuality, S/M, and falling in love.

Crystal: You know, the S/M community is probably not as sexual as the world thinks we are, because we do a lot of our S/M without sex. Yet we are a sexually free community because we can do our S/M and be sexual and not fall in love at the same time. We play. We have affairs. We do scenes, and then we can say, "Thank you very much" and walk away.

Susan: You can do one of these scenarios and be sexual with someone and not fall in love?

Crystal: Oh yeah. Definitely.

Susan: You're the only person I've ever met like that. [Laughter.]

Crystal: I'm probably the only S/M dyke that you've talked to.

Susan: How often do you suppose you do some version of a play scene with someone?

Crystal: Realistically, maybe once a week. You know, with work and jobs and your life, there's only so much time. And I don't date a lot of people at once. I do much better with one or two, max. I could see where I could be playing with one and not being sexual and where I could play with another one and be sexual.

Susan: So it would be improbable that you'd be sexual with more than one person at a time?

Crystal: Right.

Susan: And why is that?

Crystal: Well, my instant thought is, Because nobody gets that lucky!

Susan: Are there many butches and femmes in the lesbian community who aren't into S/M?

Crystal: I don't see very many of them. So much of the community has gone to androgyny, I think. Still, to this day, lipstick lesbians and butches are put down by our own community. They just won't leave us alone. The other day a butch woman was in our women's coffee shop down the street here. Another woman went up to her and said, "You make me sick. You are the kind of lesbian I wish didn't even exist." Well, that's an intense thing to say to another lesbian only because she's a butch.

Susan: When did that start, that kind of disgust with butches and femmes?

Crystal: I think with the feminist movement. And it still goes on. And what does that tell you? That we're pretty backward still.

I think butches and femmes have a wonderful history. As an old-school butch, my feelings now are that we are losing our butches. The young butches coming up, what's going to happen to them? They no longer have mentors. Are they going to just be left on the wayside as boys?

Susan: What do you mean?

Crystal: I mean that there's such a gender thing going on now. If you're not androgynous, if you're really really butch, instead of just remaining a butch woman, these women are calling themselves "boys" and taking hormones and having sex-change operations. I see young butches now and think, Oh god, you'd make a great butch. But if you call 'em a butch, they get upset. "I'm a boy! I want to be a boy."

What happened to being proud of who you are? I see that diminishing, and I think it's a shame. I am trying to hook up with the younger butch women and hopefully instill in them the honor and the integrity that there is in being a butch woman. Because it is a part of our lesbian community and our history. I think butches definitely have their place. I know there are femmes out there who really don't want to lose us.

Kay and Hannah

"Once we get into bed, it's really fun."
— Kay
"She's putty in my hands."
— Hannah

Kay: During sex Hannah will tell me stories, which I've told her I like. I can't tell Hannah stories because she can't hear me.

Susan: Hannah, what's a story you would tell Kay?

Hannah: It would be about the two of us being in a public place, and getting excited, but not having sex there, going off some place. You know, looking at each other, teasing each other, and then going off. I have the control, and Kay's very willing.

Kay: It's the sneaky part that's so exciting. There's one story about being outside on a picnic, people are passing by, and we're fooling around, touching under a blanket. Or we're in a restaurant and playing with each other under the tablecloth, so people don't know. She just makes these stories up.

Susan: And you would tell Kay one of these stories while you're making love?

Kay: Yes, it's part of making love.

Hannah: I know when to rush the story through, or when to slow the story down! I'm very in tune with Kay's body.

Kay: I like the stories a lot. I've always liked sneaky sex!

Hannah: Also, I know that every day Kay has to be in charge because of her job. It thrills me that I have control with her, that I can seduce her; she's putty in my hands!

Kay: Well, if she describes it like that, I'm not sure I like it so much!

Hannah: Maybe "putty" is the wrong word. I can lower her defenses. I feel that she really trusts me a lot.

Kay: Hannah says I have this appearance of...

Hannah: ... "stay back." I'm one of the few people that Kay doesn't have to do that with.

Kay and Hannah are in their mid-forties and have been together eleven years. We are sitting at the kitchen table of their upscale but casual two-story bungalow in Berkeley, California, drinking lattes from their own machine. Sunlight pours in the many windows, creating a warm glow as it strikes hardwood floors.

Kay is a Jewish woman, quick-spoken, with dark eyes that regard both me and Hannah intensely. Her black hair is touched with gray. She is dressed for work in a navy blue suit jacket and slacks.

Hannah is more casual, wearing a red sweatshirt and black slacks. She has round features, a clear complexion, red cheeks, and jet-black hair. Hannah has been deaf since she contracted meningitis as a six-year-old. She lip-reads with great skill and talks somewhat slowly, but Kay acts as interpreter for the interview, signing my comments and questions and her own responses, watching Hannah's gestures and translating them for me into audible words.

Hannah has graceful, extremely mobile hands, set off with bright red fingernail polish, and is active in her responses, leaning back in her chair, covering her face with her hands, throwing open her arms to accent what she feels. Kay is more contained, but vibrates with the concentration required of her role; her eyes dart from Hannah to me, her hands are continuously in motion, and — because she has to speak for both herself and Hannah — she is always talking.

Hannah: Our first kiss was wonderful, but very emotional for Kay. She cried. She didn't know if she was ready for a sexual relationship. We had been friends for about three months and were on the verge of having sex. But I was more ready than Kay was. So she said, "No." I said, "Fine," and didn't push her. Two days later she was ready.

Kay: I remember having consciously decided that I was not going to start a relationship with sex, that I was finished with that. Sex clouded my judgment. I would get involved with people, and six months later I would discover the relationship was no good.

So I didn't do that with Hannah. I wanted to wait until I felt like we had established a good friendship before I was going to have sex.

Susan: What is it about sex that had clouded your judgment?

Kay: I think people become crazy during that first six months. I've had lots of sexual partners — not relationships, just sexual partners — because sex was a lot of fun. So then I would think I was in a relationship with someone because I was seeing them a lot. But I wasn't in a relationship with them; I was just seeing them a lot. That was what was so confusing.

Susan: Tell me what happened two days after the first kiss.

Hannah: Kay came over and we were sitting around and finally she said, "Do you want to go to bed?" I thought to myself, Does she mean do I want to go to bed so she's going to leave? or, Does she want to go to bed with me? It was a very unromantic moment. I just sat there quietly until finally I understood it.

The first night of sex was very awkward; we didn't automatically fit together. I think we were too conscious of each other's movements.

Kay: Back then Hannah and I had very different ways of having sex. I think I was very comfortable with sex, and I got the feeling you, Hannah, were not comfortable.

Hannah: I don't remember. I was numb. My father had just died, so I had a lot of mixed feelings. I didn't know, really, what I was feeling. I'm trying to think . . . [Hannah pauses, and both women relax their hands, Hannah's on the table in front of her, Kay's in her lap.]

Kay's the most passionate partner I've ever had, and I think it's because I trust her. We worked on that.

Susan: What do you mean by "passionate"?

Hannah: I don't know. I don't have the words for it.

Kay: When I think about "passionate" I think of more intense or deep feelings, having more fun, maybe more willing to do things.

Hannah: I get excited with Kay in a way that I didn't

get before. Before I felt like I had to really work at getting excited, like there was a wall or something. But with Kay, that wall came down. I allowed myself to get excited.

Susan: Can you tell me about some passionate time the two of you have had together?

Hannah: Yes. It was our first vacation together, in the wine country up north of here, so, ten years ago.

Kay: I remember that, we were very passionate and sexual with each other for an hour, or two hours.

Hannah: It was like a movie.

Kay: We were really wild, rumbling around in bed, in different positions, and . . . you know. We were exhausted afterward.

Hannah: It was amazing. I never had that happen before or after. Not like that. I can easily have two orgasms when we make love, but that time, I don't know, I stopped counting.

Susan: What do you think the circumstances were that let that time happen?

Kay: I don't know what it was.

Hannah: Kay had told me she needed some space, and I was shocked because I'm the one who normally needs space. Kay said, "I just want to sleep alone one night." I felt a little bit hurt and became really quiet. I went to my bedroom — we had two bedrooms — and started reading, and then Kay came in, and we looked at each other, and it was some kind of connection. After that . . . Kay never got her space!

Kay: Once I had established some kind of territory, and it was okay to do that, I really didn't need it. I knew that there was something special in our relationship.

Hannah: It was a moment of truth.

Kay: And there was no phone, no television.

Hannah: Kay likes the phone a lot.

Kay: There were no interruptions.

Hannah: Kay has a hard time being quiet, sitting still

at home. And I have a hard time not doing something around the house. On our vacation, there was really nothing to do . . .

Kay and Hannah are smiling broadly at each other. Hannah makes a very few quick motions to Kay, and Kay signs just a couple of words in response. They both then politely turn back to me, having achieved a moment of private communication made possible by the special language they share.

Susan: Do the two of you talk about sex?

Hannah: We talk about problems that we have. We talk about feelings that we have. I talk about what excites me. I don't think I hold back.

Kay: Our sexual relationship has not been the smoothest; it's required a lot of work. It has sort of gone up and down and up and down and up and down forever.

Hannah: It's very hard for me to get to the point of having sex. I have a lot of garbage, so getting there is a problem for me. Then when we're having sex, it's fine. I'm always thinking, Why don't I allow myself to get there? And I don't know. That's always been a hard part of the relationship for me, with everyone I've been with, not just Kay.

Kay: Also our timing is very different. I'm a morning and afternoon kind of person, Hannah is very much of the night. She stays awake until one or two o'clock, so about eleven o'clock she's ready to have sex. Well, at eleven o'clock I am sound asleep, or should be sound asleep. I don't have any energy at that time.

Hannah: I wonder if the timing is one way for me to sabotage . . . I don't know if I'm a night person as a way of avoiding sex. Although there's something about the dark and candles that's really exciting to me. And I need a lot of stimulation to get into the mood; during the day there's no stimulation. So it's a mixture of influences, but sex is a lot of work.

Kay: Also we don't often sleep together in the same room because Hannah has such a bad snoring problem, and I have sleeping problems. So that's not a good combination. But she had surgery two weeks ago, and I think we will start sleeping together regularly. It's a big issue in our life.

Susan: So how do you get yourselves to have sex?

Kay: Well, the last time we had sex was this past Sunday. It was the afternoon, so Hannah figured I was going to cooperate. We're very practical, we say, "Do you want to go up and make love?" It's not like trying to seduce the other person ahead of time because that doesn't work for me; I'm never sure if it's really going to happen. So I've made the decision just to say, "Do you want to do it now? Is this a good time? Are you in the mood? Can you get in the mood?" Then I get an answer, and after that, if we do it, it's really fun.

Hannah: I need to lie down and talk and connect, not just look at each other and dive into bed. So we lie in bed and talk and connect and laugh. We do that for a while before we actually start making love. I love that part. That's the foreplay for me, the talking and the laughing.

Susan: Who would be more likely to bring up having sex?

Hannah: We bring it up equally, but Kay brings it up when the time is better for her; then I accept it more. When I bring it up, it's most often late at night, not a good time for Kay. So 90 percent of the time Kay says no.

Susan: How often do you suppose you make love, on the average?

Hannah: This month we've had it twice, which is doing really good for us. Sometimes we've gone for a month, two months without having sex or making love.

Susan: What do you think affects how often you make love?

Hannah: For a while it was me, my garbage from the past. Then I started working on the issues, and Kay started menopause, and it was like, I'm ready, where's Kay? Now I'm horny a lot, a *lot,* and Kay's not. I believe that we're really intimate, and really like each other. I'm never bored with Kay, I'm very entertained by her. But I do think if we weren't that way, I'd be really angry about our sex life.

Kay: I'm not sure how much of it is that I gave up because it was such a struggle before, and how much of it is hormonal. But I know I used to love to masturbate, and I don't even do that very much. And I don't think that's connected to the struggle with Hannah, which tells me that it's really chemical.

I guess I have to just decide that even if I don't feel like being sexual, I know it will be fun once we're in bed. But I don't think about sex very much any more. I don't think about bringing it up because I don't have the feeling.

Hannah: For me sex became less important when we became more emotionally intimate. And that was a relief for me. I'd rather have emotional intimacy than sex once a week and have the relationship be very superficial.

And I don't think of cheating on Kay like I would have in the past. Now, if I want to have sex with somebody else because I'm feeling more sexual, I think, What would be the impact on our relationship? I'm concerned about Kay's feelings. In the past I couldn't do that; it was all about me.

Susan: Do you have an agreement about being monogamous?

Kay: Absolutely. Hannah and I made a decision within the first year that we would not go off and have sexual relationships with other people.

I was not a monogamous person when we met. I also

had never had a really serious relationship, except for one time, when I ended up kind of sneaking off, and that was the end.

Now I realize that doing that was more just for sex, and as sex has become less important to me, that need has also become less important.

I also believe strongly that relationships do not do well when people are having sex with other people outside of the relationship. I have not seen one relationship survive that. And I wanted this relationship to be permanent.

Sometimes we get mad at each other and threaten, but I never did it, and I trust Hannah never did it.

Susan: Can you tell me some funny story about being sexual?

Hannah: Oh yes. One time in Kay's old apartment we were close to having an orgasm at the same time, and all of a sudden the lights went out. It was like, oh my god! There went our joint orgasm! And then at the same time, we were hysterical, it was so funny. That was one of the best ones.

Kay: I don't remember that, actually. Since menopause, we have to rely on Hannah's memory.

Hannah: I'm the memory for us.

Susan: You're the couple historian.

Hannah: You bet. I take the pictures too. And I'm the social planner.

Kay: I'll tell a funny story. We were selling Hannah's condo, we had it on the market, and it had one of those lock boxes for the realtor to use when she wanted to show the place. She always called first, and Hannah would run around and clean up everything. Well, one night we had been using my vibrator, and there was underwear on the floor. The next morning I left for work, Hannah was in the living room, and the realtor and this woman who had seen the condo about fifteen times walked in, "Is it okay if I just look around again?" After the two women left,

Hannah ran into the bedroom and there, right in the middle of the floor, was this vibrator . . .

Hannah: . . . with my bra lying on the floor next to it.

Kay: The woman never came back.

Susan: Do you like any other sex toys besides vibrators?

Hannah: I don't like a vibrator. It's too fast.

Kay: I like a vibrator.

Hannah: Other than that, we've had no toys. I'm too embarrassed to go into a sex-toy store. I would look at the floor the whole time, sure everyone is watching me. I buy erotic books though, you know, nice stories, not porn.

Susan: Lesbian erotica?

Kay: And straight erotica too.

Hannah: I'm not interested in gay men, but three people, two women and a man, that's fine. I'm flexible.

Susan: Can you tell me what it is you particularly like to do sexually?

Kay: I love kissing. I think kissing is the most wonderful invention. Mostly I like kissing on the lips, the mouth lips, because . . . I don't know . . . lips are so wonderful.

Hannah: And we're good kissers too.

Kay: I like to be kissed all over. I like to be touched pretty much all over. And I like to go really slow; I like to take time.

Hannah: I like to talk, less touching. It has to be just the right time for me to be able to be touched and not be ticklish. I like pretty much everything, though I don't like to be touched in my anus. That's off limits, and we don't do that.

Kay: I had experience with anal intercourse when I was straight, and I actually liked it, but we don't do that. We do oral sex; I love that a lot. Hannah seems to love that a lot.

Hannah: We don't have orgasms at the same time.

Kay: Our timing is different. I'm much slower to get to orgasm. Hannah almost always has an orgasm first, then I have one. It's a turn-on for me to watch her or listen to her have an orgasm; it's part of my foreplay.

Susan: What's the most unconventional thing you do sexually?

Kay: Hmmm.

Hannah: Nothing. We don't tie each other up.

Kay: I'm not sure that's very unconventional now!

Hannah: We just started talking about getting a dildo. That would be unconventional for me, and for Kay too. I like vaginal penetration, and Kay doesn't do it very often. And although she doesn't like that for herself, last week she said, "I think you would like it."

Kay: I was thinking about it because, although you're a lesbian, I know you liked sex with men because you liked that kind of penetration. But then I was thinking about it some more, driving to work yesterday, and I don't know if I would feel good about doing that. I think in some ways I would feel like I was being a fake man. And that would not feel comfortable. I don't know if I could wear a fake penis, basically.

Hannah: I don't know if I would be comfortable either. We're not going to know until we try it and become hysterical, which will probably happen.

Susan: Can you tell me how your being deaf, Hannah, affects your being sexual, if it does?

Hannah: It's very important for me to have other lesbians know I'm sexual. I want them to see this deaf person and know that I'm sexual too, just like them. Some people see the deafness and can't see beyond it.

My deafness is really important to me; it's an important identity. But for other people, deafness is a disability. For me, it's a culture, more like an ethnic group.

Kay: Deafness is a culture because there's a language,

American Sign Language, and because they have rules within their community, and they have norms, how you're supposed to behave. So the deaf people that Hannah hangs out with professionally all think of themselves as a culture, not as a disability. They don't see it as something terribly wrong physically with the person. They understand that there will be problems, that it's a hard life, in a way. But if a deaf person has a child, they want their kid to be deaf, they want to pass on the culture.

Hannah: I think in the past, the narrowness of the deaf community made it hard for me to feel comfortable being a lesbian. So I had to hide it for a really long time, and pretend like I was straight, and all that. But I'm not in the closet any more.

Kay: Hannah is a professional, highly educated deaf person. But the general deaf community is not highly educated, many leave high school, many don't read English very well. So if there's a connection between attitudes about sex and your educational level, which I think there probably is, a culture with lower-educated people, like deaf culture, will be a bit more narrow.

Susan: Earlier in the interview, Hannah, you talked about having issues about being sexual. Do any of them have to do with being deaf?

Hannah: No. Not at all. They're connected to my growing up and my garbage and my Lutheran religious upbringing.

Susan: Do either of you think your being deaf, Hannah, affects how you actually do sex?

Hannah: Yes. For instance, I have to have the lights on. I don't do anything in the dark, because that's no fun. I have nothing to hide and don't have that inhibition.

Kay: I've always liked to have the lights on. If the lights are off, Hannah basically becomes deaf-blind, which is pretty scary. And if I want to talk with her, I can't do that with the lights off.

Hannah: My being deaf means that I'm the one that's doing most of the talking during sex.

Kay: We have two choices for me to communicate with Hannah: Either I use sign language or Hannah lip-reads me. Neither of which works if I'm trying to kiss her, or do oral sex, or whatever. Also I enjoy listening to Hannah moaning and making noise — it's very exciting — so I feel bad that she can't hear me.

Hannah: It's hard to lip-read while Kay's moaning! Of course not being able to hear her, I really don't know what I'm missing.

I think Kay has become better at using her body to tell me things. But I wish she would be more physical during orgasm because, since I'm a visual person, I don't know if it was good or not. I get confused because the physical response doesn't match what I think it should look like. Afterward Kay will say, "That was great," and I'll be shocked. It's like talking to someone who says, "I'm so happy," but they're not smiling.

I often have to ask Kay how she feels, because she puts on a mask during the day.

Kay: Sometimes my mood and Hannah's interpretation of it is wrong.

Hannah: If I was hearing, I could hear her voice. Her tone and the words she uses tell people whether they can come close or should stay away. Kay's expressions are very hard to read.

Susan: You must be more visual than hearing people are.

Hannah: Yes, yes. I know when something in the house has been moved. I can see a bug a mile away. I'm very aware of what's going on in the environment.

Kay: Sometimes it's like she has eyes in the back of her head. It's a little scary.

Susan: Because you're more visual, do you especially like how Kay looks?

Hannah: I think she's a gorgeous woman, but sometimes she wears shit clothes. I just want to rip them off.

Kay: But you don't want to rip them off and have sex!

Hannah: No, but sometimes I like to sit back and admire you. [Hannah does sit back and smiles at Kay.]

You know, I was thinking, the better Kay learns my language, American Sign Language, the better it is in bed too.

Kay: Oh, why is that?

Hannah: Because you depend less on me looking at you to read your words. The more skilled you become with sign language, the better you are at communicating with me in other ways that are nonverbal.

Susan: Kay, when you were first getting to know Hannah, and beginning to be in love, did you think about, What is it going to mean to have a relationship with someone who is deaf?

Kay: I don't think that's how I think about things. I was just so excited about this new person. And I had had some contact with deaf people, so it wasn't a totally strange thing to me. Being in a relationship with Hannah has changed my life a lot, and I would say it's all basically positive. It's been a gift.

Hannah: A gift, huh?

Kay: Well, sure. I think your being in a relationship with a Jew is my gift to you, right?

Susan: Do you think being Jewish has any impact on your sexuality?

Kay: Well, I grew up in a nonsexual household. I didn't get *any* messages from my parents about sex, whether negative or positive. I mean, I'm surprised they had children! My parents didn't like each other very much.

I think that I have more open attitudes about sex, and that's connected to being Jewish, because basically Jewish culture is a very liberal political culture. In Jewish law the husband and wife are supposed to sexually satisfy each other. Jewish culture and religion don't have the attitude that sex is only for marriage. So I didn't grow up with stuff about damnation and only having sex because you want to have a baby.

Being a lesbian was no big deal either. The Jewish community — at least the non-Orthodox Jewish community — is very clear about the difference between your rights and your personal life. And, being a minority, they understand what it can mean if your rights are taken away.

The sun's rays are now pouring through the south-facing windows of Kay and Hannah's home, our lattes are long gone, and both women need to head off for work soon. There is time for just a few more questions.

Susan: If you were going to change something about your sexual lives, what would you most want to change?

Kay: I would like to get back my sexual energy. That would be the first thing. I like the feeling of being turned on, so that's what I miss. And then I would want to have sex more and on a regular basis. When I don't have sex regularly, I don't feel like having sex regularly. When I have it regularly, I want it more.

Our sexual relationship has been such hard work that I haven't wanted to struggle any more, so I also think I've become mentally lazy. But I don't need to feel turned on in order to have sex. I think Hannah and I need to find a compromise time that's not exactly my time, and not exactly her time. I need not to think of excuses not to be sexual. And not get so busy that somehow sex gets way down the priority list. I think it's a decision, to be more sexual.

Hannah: I need to practice saying "yes" more. I need to push myself. The last two times Kay asked me, at first I said, "No, no, no," and I was kind of sad, so then I said, "Okay, let's go do it." I'd like to do sex more often. Once a week, at least.

Kay: And I would like longer sex.

Hannah: I notice that we talk more, so for me it seems longer, but for Kay it seems shorter.

Kay: I wouldn't reduce the talking part; I would just increase the time focused on sex.

Susan: Do the two of you feel different in terms of intimacy if you're being sexual?

Kay: I feel more connected with Hannah.

Hannah: I have a glow for a while. [Hannah is smiling broadly at me.]

Kay: But, Hannah [Kay reaches over and taps Hannah on the arm], do you have a glow because you physically feel better, or because of the connection, or both?

Hannah: The connection. But I get a glow from just talking to Kay too. Like last week we lay in bed for five hours and just talked. That was very powerful for me. So I get a glow from that too; I can have that feeling without sex.

Susan: What would it accomplish for you, if you were sexual more?

Hannah: I feel a little bit not normal. I think I should be doing it once a week; it sounds like the right thing to do. And when we do it, it's so much fun, so I wonder why it is we put it off.

Kay: I think it would be adding more fun in our life, which is something I need in my life anyway. It's a high. I can get high exercising. I can get high going to a good movie. I can get high eating good food. And sex has its own special high.

Also, when we've had sex, there is a special kind of connection that I don't experience otherwise. It's not that it's more intimate. But I feel softer. It's a loving feeling that I don't feel outside of sex.

Sex creates an enclosed moment, where it's just the two of us, where there's not a world outside.

It makes me feel like the world's okay.

Rita

"I'm learning that I have a hungry
appetite for sexual contact."

My family was very traditional. For my grandmother, who was born in Mexico and immigrated to the United States, bodies were used strictly for working the fields and sex for procreation. For my mother's generation, raised in the United States under the influence of mainstream, white America, things started slowly to change and to create conflict between mothers and daughters. My mother changed her style of dress and style of hair, she began to use makeup, she listened to different music and used different language.

For me, being been born in the 1950s and being a teenager in the 1960s changed the way I viewed sexuality. It changed my comfort with sex and my being able to express it in language. I experienced "coming in touch with my feelings." For my mother's generation or my grandmother's or my great-grandmother's, that wasn't important, to come in touch with anything. Except the soil.

Rita and I are talking in the attic studio she has claimed as a space for herself in an otherwise unremarkable house in a St. Louis suburb. Downstairs her three children are entertaining friends in the family room, but upstairs we are alone, cut off from collective life, surrounded by materials that manifest Rita's distinctive personality, interests, and passions.

Her desk and computer and files are here, spilling over with notes and papers from her graduate-school life. Her Buddhist altar is along one wall, evidence of new spiritual paths adopted by this once-Catholic woman. Her queen-size bed fills one corner, ringed by flowers and candles, the place she sleeps alone or welcomes her girlfriend. There are photographs of her mother and her aunts, her children and other family members, and one small picture of her girlfriend. There are green plants and a red, green, and yellow light wool Mexican rug thrown over a wicker chair.

The room is full of rich primary colors, vibrant like its creator, a short, full-figured, forty-five-year-old woman, with shoulder-length flyaway black and gray hair. Rita says her room represents her attempt to live an integrated life, a life of spiritual consciousness, economic moderation, political commitment, emotional growth, and sexual expression.

Susan: What message did you get from your family about being sexual?

Rita: The message was that you just don't talk about it, whatever "it" is. We didn't talk about menstruation, we didn't talk about sex with a spouse, we just didn't talk about it.

Susan: So how did you learn about sex?

Rita: I just learned on my own, through trial and error.

I think I was different at a very young age, and I knew it, but I never acted on it. The price would have been too high. In my culture there were only two kinds of women, a heterosexual woman and a mother. Everybody outside that did not fit into real-woman behavior.

Susan: Why did you think you were different?

Rita: When I was about seven or eight I lived next door to a girl from Mexico, a twelve-year-old. She was very mannish, very strong, very appealing. We played together all the time, and we touched each other quite a bit, though never any inappropriate touch. She would protect me from other children and hold me close and carry me everywhere, like a mother carrying a child. I really enjoyed it. I felt very natural in her arms.

Susan: Did her touch feel sexual?

Rita: It did feel sexual, insofar as I could understand what "sexual" felt like at that age. I always wanted to be with her, only with her. Then in my teen years certain types of women attracted me, women who were very independent, who stood out, who were leaders of their own life.

Nonetheless I started dating boys when I was about fourteen or fifteen. Being gay is taboo in Mexican culture. The terms used to denigrate gay people are cruel and vicious. I must have made a decision somewhere along the line that I could not take that kind of harassment, that that was not a road I would take.

Susan: You knew lesbians were a type of person that existed?

Rita: Yes, but the type of person you kept away from. I knew I couldn't pursue that kind of life. I just detached from it emotionally.

Susan: If you started to feel something for a woman, would it be a red flag for you?

Rita: Yeah, and I'd feel guilty, that I should not have that feeling.

Susan: And what was the feeling?

Rita: The feeling was that I was being aroused by her presence.

I think my mother always knew that I was different too. I thought differently, I moved differently, I dressed differently. I went to a Catholic school where the girls wore white tops and wool skirts and sweaters. I wore my uniform, but also a vampire coat and Mexican sandals and black sunglasses. In fact, as the years went on, we laughed about it. But at the time she tried to temper that part of me so I wouldn't have to suffer. Mexican women are modest, very temperate in their manners and their behavior. Better for all women to look the same, act the same, be the same. This way you don't stand out, you're not the object of ridicule. She didn't want me to suffer by being too visible.

Susan: By being too visible as what?

Rita: As a woman, as a woman of color, as someone who was different, who looked different and dressed different. Such people are always cause for suspicion. So my mother always tried to temper me, in my dress, my manners, my behavior, everything.

Susan: So were you a virgin when you got married?

Rita: No. I lost my virginity to a young man in high school when I was a sophomore or junior. He was very good-looking and came from an upper-middle-class Mexican business family. Our relationship lasted for two years, but we never really communicated very well. That first introduction to sex was very abusive. Sex was not something he asked for; sex was something he demanded. My comfort was not important. And at the end, if I didn't produce satisfaction, I got a heavy verbal bashing. I learned to feel guilty at a young age about my inability to perform.

Susan: What were you supposed to have done?

Rita: Enjoyed it. Played with it. Satisfied him, whichever way he wanted. But I was resisting. I was learning how to establish boundaries with men. My father left when I was three months old because my mother kicked him out. Then I had a stepfather who was emotionally abusive. So I had come to a place where there was very little I was willing to tolerate from men. Later, a friend taught me exactly how to put them in their place. When men look at you in a sexual way, like they're sizing you up, you look down at their penis. It works all the time. You dethrone them because they're not used to being looked at as sexual objects. They can't handle it.

Sex was painful for me. There were physiological reasons for that, but also I thought, That's it? All this big hype for that? I learned at an early age that something wasn't quite right. Still, I had been raised that my job was always to satisfy the man. But I never felt like I was getting anything out of it. Instead I learned to be on guard, to calculate what it was I was going to get from a situation, what I was going to give the situation, and who I was going to interact with. My partner tells me now, "Rita, when you go into a room you have certain expectations, and if they're not met, you let everybody know it."

I did not really want to get married. I was avoiding it and didn't get married until I was twenty-eight. But then I met a man who seemed like a nice person, he had a good job, stability, prestige, all the qualities we're brainwashed to think are important. He seemed to have sure values about life, he was mature, and my family was pressuring me.

Susan: Were you in love with him?

Rita: I loved him as a human being. I don't think I was in love with him. In fact we almost didn't get married because I saw red flags while we were courting, warnings that he was sexually not my type; he was too passive. It was a reflection of his very deep Catholic upbringing; he viewed sex as something dirty. It was a scar that carried over into our bedroom. He wasn't creative, he didn't feel comfortable exploring different ways to be sexual. He could only do it missionary style. And orgasm was a big component. "Did you reach orgasm?" He wanted to know, was he doing his part? And most of the time I just lied, to get him off my back.

It's hard to know if we had a good sex life, but I don't think we ever did. We had children right after we got married, so we never spent much time working on our relationship. But I was married for seventeen years, until two years ago I decided that that was it.

Susan: What changed to lead you to that decision?

Rita: My mother. In one respect my mother was very traditional, telling me you had to stay in the marriage for the sake of the family. But in another respect she was very contemporary, she was saying, "I want you to think for yourself." My mother has been a powerful force in my life; she was instrumental in helping me come out as the woman that I am now, although I'm still emerging. I grew watching my mother stretch and open up her own understanding about who she was.

As my mother was kind of retraining herself and retraining me it was frightening. But because I trusted her so, I became more independent, and things that lay dormant began to out. To be independent meant I should live my life the way I felt my life should be led. And that did not include being married.

Susan: You're very close to your mother.

Rita: Yes. She just passed away a few weeks ago. [I am shocked by this news and say how sorry I am that her mother is dead; Rita nods and continues.] That's okay. She was seventy years old. My mother and I did a lot of lifework. We battled through everything, we challenged ourselves, we really grew. It was an unusual relationship. Yes, we are very close, my mother and I.

A silence falls upon us, and Rita and I take a few deep breaths. She gets up from her chair, walks across the room, and comes back with the picture of her mother and her two aunts. Her mother looks strikingly like an older version of Rita herself.

Rita: It was because of my mom and my aunts that I began to come out as a lesbian. I would go to Arizona to visit and would sit with my aunts and my mom and ask them questions, about how they felt about their lives, and if they had it to do over, what would they have done differently? Three years ago they said, "You live your life, Rita, the way you want to. So you don't have any regrets by the time you are our age."

I took it to heart. On my next visit I let them know I was a lesbian, and proud of it, and very political and still growing into it. One aunt was immediately accepting, and the other, who is a very right-wing Christian, is learning to handle it. My mom was very accepting of me, but was not accepting of my partner. But before she died, she blessed our relationship. She said to my partner, "Take care of my daughter and my grandchildren."

Susan: When did you meet your partner?

Rita: We met at the Gay Pride parade, introduced by a mutual friend. I was attracted to her because she was a Chicana; I was interested in pursuing friendships only with other Chicanas, of whom there are very few here. We developed a friendship, and were respectful of each other's turf and boundaries. We waited until her relationship with a woman back home was over, and we went slowly, because our intent was to weave a blanket of friendship.

Susan: How did you get from being friends to being lovers? Can you describe your first kiss?

Rita: Of course I can, Susan!

Susan: *Will* you describe your first kiss?

Rita: No, I will not! [Rita has an attack of modesty here, but quickly recovers.] All right. [A small smile appears.] Getting to the kiss took months, it was very gradual, a big buildup. It was a very slow kiss, not aggressive. She didn't dominate the kiss, although she was a veteran dyke. But I'm a real good student; I know what to learn!

Susan: Was kissing her idea?

Rita: I thought it was her idea. She says I prepped her up, she says, "Just by your manner, the way you are."

It's been a very easy friendship. Our family backgrounds are similar, our parents' experiences are similar, our values and what we aspire to as women are very similar. But we are different women emotionally. I was used to feeling. My mother taught me later on in life not to be afraid of emotions. It was okay to feel happy, but it was also okay to feel rage and anger and to feel sad and to cry. But my partner is very contained and is not comfortable with feelings, so we've been able to teach each other. She's been a very good student about feelings.

Susan: When was the first time you were sexual together?

Rita: It was at her home. It was very scary for me; it

had taken a long time to build trust. I've had only two committed relationships in my life, my husband and now my partner. I'm not excited by affairs and one-night stands. When I open up my heart to you, I'm giving it all to you, and you need to be solid enough in yourself to take care of it and not abuse it.

Also, I need to be able to give a partner my respect. Respect is not passing judgments on her views. Respect is giving space for her to evolve and grow, not to control or hamper her. Respect is working on myself so I am aware of my behavior toward her.

So I don't move quickly. I take a lot of time.

I observed her. I watched out for red flags because I don't want to be involved with someone unless they're doing lifework. Because how they are impacts me, and that impacts my children, and I'm very protective of myself and the children. I don't want people in my circle who are sloppy with their lives, who are not active in pursuing their own growth. I don't want to have the burden of carrying their weight, I need a woman who is paving her own way. So I told her I was observing her, that she was on probation.

Susan: Probation for what?

Rita: For something more intimate.

Susan: What happened the first night you made love?

Rita: We used to spend time lying with each other and cuddling, getting used to each other's body temperature and smells. We were very slow exploring each other's bodies; it was really quite beautiful. She was very patient. She was very slow and tender. Very loving. A real pro!

I realized almost immediately that I had sure wasted a lot of years with my husband. There was a level of communication I had never experienced with a man. I wasn't there to satisfy her; we were there to satisfy each other. And that satisfaction was not just sexual. It was touch, it could have been a sisterly embrace, it was the way we spoke, it was the way we reassured each other that we were not there to scar one another. It was very different. And I knew that it was very natural for me.

Susan: Did you make love to her too?

Rita: I made love to her too. She taught me how. We had a deal. She would be a good teacher, and I would be a good student.

Susan: What are some of the things you and she like to do together sexually?

Rita: She likes to put her fist inside of me. She gets real excited about that because after my having had three babies, it's real easy for her to do that to me. And if I'm in the right frame of mind, if my body's relaxed, it's okay. If not, it's very painful for me, so I have to let her know right away whether that's okay for her to do or not. And she likes to have full control of my breasts, all the time. I'm used to having kids, but I'm not used to having a strong, powerful woman on me all the time.

Susan: She likes to suck on your nipples . . . ?

Rita: Constantly! Constantly! It could be an all-day thing, you know? You can find humor in all this, but I also think it's very necessary for her to be close to me like a little girl sometimes. We've given each other permission to be just about anything we want, little girls or rowdy teenagers, sophisticated young adults with an attitude, mature women.

Susan: Is there anything about butch and femme in any of this?

Rita: Yes, there is. But being a new kid on the block here, all the old definitions of what butch-femme is are kind of silly to me. I just go with my natural instincts about how I am. I love the drama of lipstick and wild hair. I love lace so I wear black lace all the time. It's very seductive to me. And push-up bras and crotchless panties. It's all very lovely. Satin and candles. It feeds into the romantic side of me.

My partner should be someone who is very *macha*, someone who can appreciate the lace in me. I like to be the lacy one in the group, this is my show. Her job is to be a good audience. My girlfriend is very butch; she wears Hanes underwear and a tank top.

Susan: Tell me about some recent favorite time you had being sexual.

Rita: I was in a really doggy-style kind of mood, you know? I was into really hard-feeling sex. I like to be on my stomach with my butt up in the air, and I like her to put her fist inside me. It's a hard thrust that I really enjoy. Her fingers are beautiful, so long and slender that she can put a whole fist inside and it's not painful. It's very smooth. And she understands my insides so well that she knows where the hot spots are.

Susan: Do you like oral sex?

Rita: I do, but I've got a thing about cleanliness. I require that she be clean and I be clean before I have oral sex.

Susan: Would she make the same requirement?

Rita: No, she doesn't worry about it. That raises questions for me, like, how comfortable am I with my body and her body? And I say, Well, I'm comfortable, but I'm not *that* comfortable.

We enjoy foreplay, which comes for us on so many levels, eye contact, a tender word, body language. There are times when I'm in a very tender mood, and I need her to be gentle. There are other times I need a rough playmate. Sometimes when I've been working hard, many, many hours, and am totally tensed up, I need a strong release. She's very good that way.

I love to be romanced and I love to be dominated by her. Because she has a very polished way of doing that. She might say to me, "You know, you belong to me. You know you're mine." That's foreplay for her, because she knows that turns me on. If a man were to say that to me,

I would feel immediately violated and tensed up. But I want to feel like I do belong to someone, and her way of communicating that to me makes me feel that I have nothing to worry about, that I do belong to her. Because I'm not open to a nonmonogamous relationship. That is too sloppy for me.

On the other hand, I'm just learning how to make love to her. I don't think I have an understanding yet about her body. Not having had babies, she's so tiny, so tight. I feel like I'm hurting her when I penetrate her. But she says, "No, you're fine." Still, I worry about it.

It's funny how she defines that. If she penetrates me, she feels we're both making love with each other. Sometimes, though, I ask myself, was she really as satisfied as I was from this? But I'm learning that my partner's satisfaction comes in different ways, not always sexually. Her satisfaction comes from being fed — I love to cook for her — and from my caring about her — "Did you take your vitamins?" "What do you need today?" There are different ways that she feels fed.

My ways are more defined. She always reminds me that I have an insatiable appetite. I'm very comfortable in telling her when I'm hungry. I just say, "I'm so hungry. You need to feed me now!" I think her arousal comes from seeing me satisfied. That's what I'm getting from her. And that works for me just fine, because I've always seen myself as the queen anyway. So it seems to work for us.

Susan: How do you think being Chicana influences how you are sexually?

Rita: I really stay with my own, with other Chicana women. There are women outside my own that I find attractive, but I wouldn't pursue them because I know that we can only get so far; after that we're not communicating on the same level.

Also women who view me as exotic, that's a major turn-off. That's an indicator to me that they're not tuned into themselves, that they rely on stereotypes. I don't like women like that.

I think my sexuality as a Chicana is highly political because I'm not only challenging the dominant society's views about who I should be as a woman, I'm also doing battle with my own culture, a culture that is very insensitive to women and especially to lesbians. They just assume that we do not exist.

I think in the twenty-first century women of color are going to be making things very uncomfortable. Being a lesbian is going to help me do that; because of it, I'm developing a voice. My identity as a lesbian — being a free woman — is very powerful for me. Coming out is the most powerful move I've ever made in my life.

Lucy

"We tried every position in the book
Loving Women. Some of them were
very complicated."

Lucy: Dana has been my partner now for nineteen
years. But before we got together she was my supervisor at
this nonprofit agency where I was an intern. When she
would supervise me, she always thought I was in such
deep concentration, listening attentively to her every word.
Actually I was staring at her breasts and thinking, Wow,
are they really that nice and soft and creamy, or what?
She always wore these little V-necked sweaters and leaned

forward to talk to me. It was like, "I'm supposed to look you in the eye? Give me a break, woman."

I had this vision, that she would hire me, and then we'd get to be friends, and then we'd get to be roommates, and then we'd get to be lovers. And she did hire me, and we got to be friends, so I knew lovers was coming, I just had to be patient. I thought since she was older and white, she knew about these kinds of things and would figure it out. I just had to be in the right place at the right time. But she didn't figure it out. It was very frustrating.

Lucy and I are talking in the corner of a group room in a Denver battered women's shelter where she works as clinical director. We are sitting in plaid overstuffed chairs, shabby from much use, the tape recorder poised on a hassock pulled up in front of us. It is six o'clock in the evening, the regular work day over, and a coworker has just taken Lucy's order for a take-out supper of barbecued ribs, baked beans, and hush puppies.

Lucy is a forty-one-year-old African-American woman, not tall but of very large proportions. She is wearing navy blue slacks and a loose-fitting overblouse, patterned in an abstract design of interwoven blue and purple circles. Her large glasses give her a slightly owl-like look. She sits quietly, her body self-contained, her hands folded properly in her lap, but her eyes sparkle, betraying the immense enjoyment she finds in recounting tales of her sexual life.

Susan: When you were growing up, how did you first hear about sex?

Lucy: My first conscious memory of sex was when I was about six, and my grandmother was talking to some old auntie or other. She said, "Never have sex with a woman, because you'll never want to have sex with a man again." I didn't know what sex was, but it did seem significant.

Susan: Do you think your grandmother was speaking from experience?

Lucy: They discussed this so authoritatively that I always wondered, but I don't think so. I certainly never had the courage to ask her. The first time she met my partner Dana, though, she asked, "Well, would you like to sleep together or in separate rooms?" My mother was having heart failure, and my sister was hyperventilating, but my grandmother, who was eighty by then, was very matter-of-fact. I had sent her a picture of Dana and me, and she said, "She's a very handsome woman." And I said, "Yeah, Grandma, I rather think so too." Her motto was, "If it suits you, it suits me."

When I was young my grandfather used to say that I acted like this old woman, Cosey Fox. Finally I asked, "Who the hell is old Cosey Fox?" And my grandfather says, "She's a bull dyke." I was just a little kid and wasn't sure what a bull dyke was, but I knew I wasn't supposed to be like that. One day Cosey Fox came down the street. I thought I was going to see a woman with horns and a tail and red eyes, but she looked like a nice enough woman.

Susan: What did your grandfather mean, that you were just like her?

Lucy: That I wasn't submissive. I didn't rebel, but I just quietly didn't do what he wanted me to do. He had this thing that women should agree with him, but even as a little kid I thought it was just the damnedest thing, because he was often wrong, and I knew he was wrong, so why would I agree with him? He would go crazy, and want to spank me, but I would run all over the neighborhood and laugh. It would just piss him off because he could never catch me, so he'd give off a shout, "You're going to be just like old Cosey Fox!"

Susan: What else did you learn from your family about sex?

Lucy: My mom was very clear about protecting me, my sister, and my two brothers from sexual abuse. She said that if someone touched us in a way that we didn't like, or touched any of our private parts, that we were to come and tell her right away, and she would believe us, and do something about it. The possibility of sexual abuse was always present in our lives, something that we kind of took for granted, that we might be accosted or that there were funny uncles or dirty old men. It was just a fact of life.

This friend of my grandfather's owned a store, so one time I went there to get some candy. I was just developing breasts, and he came in and started pinching them. I said, "Don't do that, that hurts." And he said, "Why not? If you let me do that, I'll give you all the candy you want." But I said, "I don't want you to do that, it hurts, and I don't care if I don't get any candy. I'm going to tell my mom." He said, "She won't believe you." And I said, "Yes, she will."

I went home, and the first person I saw was my grandfather, so I told him. He said, "Don't tell your mom, because he'll lose his job. Let's just keep it between you and me." And I thought, "This is bullshit." So I went and told my mother. And he lost his job.

In my family we had real frank talks about sex and venereal disease and why you don't want to get pregnant at thirteen, and what would happen if you did, that is, about abortion. Middle-class black girls did not get pregnant out of wedlock, and if you did, you certainly did not have the baby and bring shame on the family. There were condoms around. And my mom was very clear about where to look if a guy told you he had a vasectomy. When my sister said, "What if it's dark?" my mom got us these little keychain flashlights [Lucy laughs]. So there was never any excuse not to know. Nor was there any excuse to get pregnant.

Susan: Were you sexual at all as a teenager?

Lucy: Are you kidding? We were so terrified, none of us experimented with early sexuality. And there was no mystery about it, so, what's the big deal?

When I was about twenty-one I was convinced that I was the world's oldest virgin so I decided to pick a guy and lose my virginity. And a likely suspect came along, so I did. He couldn't believe it, that I was a virgin. He said, "I can't do this?" I said, "Why not?" He said, "I just can't. It's going to shrivel up." I said, "You're the one I chose, so carry on." And he did, but he was quite shook up about it.

We had a relationship for a year. He was a nice guy. I wasn't in love with him, but he was handy as a boyfriend and decent sexually; he kind of satisfied those needs. He was fun to have sex with, I enjoyed it.

Susan: What did you like about it?

Lucy: I realized that I didn't like penetration as much as I liked all the foreplay. I liked oral sex. I liked all of it. I didn't do anything too kinky, but I thought it was fun. But I was far more interested in sex than he was. He said, "I'm never going to screw a virgin again. You really should warn a guy."

Susan: Did you have sex with other men too?

Lucy: I decided I really should experiment a little, but you could count them on one hand and not use your thumb.

Susan: And when did women enter the picture?

Lucy: I think I've always been attracted to women. I was coming of age right when the women's movement started, so the "L" word was being bandied about. So I knew there were lesbians, but I didn't know any. It was in the back of my mind that I might be one, but I wasn't sure, because I really did enjoy sex with men.

So I decided to start reading. *Patience and Sarah* was the first book, which was singularly unhelpful. I looked up "lesbian" in the encyclopedia and tried to find things in bookstores, but they were always clinical, you know, about the causes of it. Which is why two women friends and I decided to start the library at the women's center that was attached to the university here. Gretchen ordered everything that had "anarchist" in the title, and Marybeth ordered everything that had "feminist" in the title, and I ordered everything that had "lesbian" in the title. I read a whole lot; I did serious research.

Susan: What do you remember being most helpful?

Lucy: Lesbian Woman by Del Martin and Phyllis Lyon. I was real comforted knowing that there were other women out there. Though not any black ones, I was convinced of that. Except for old Cosey Fox, of course, and she was bad.

And *Loving Women* by the Nomadic Sisters, which was very good about the technical aspects of things, about exactly how to do it. It had nice little drawings. I cherished that book.

Susan: Do you remember a favorite picture from it?

Lucy: I remember two women, with long hair, one lying on top of the other, nibbling at her girlfriend's breast. When Dana and I finally got together we tried every position in that book!

Susan: How did Dana and you get together?

Lucy: Well, once I started to get a little more information from all my reading, I began to name the feelings I was having, I began to realize that I was very attracted to Dana. She had hired me once my internship was over, and I loved being around her at work, I loved being in the office, I watched her all the time. Sometimes I would think, How can she not know? But she was just oblivious.

Then she asked me if I wanted to be her roommate, and I thought, heck yes, my vision is coming true, so I moved in with her.

My first day there I'm using the bathroom, taking a piss, and she comes in! I was shocked, I mean, white girls are so brazen, they have no sense of decency. I said, "I am in here." She said, "It doesn't bother me." I thought, "Oh my god." She runs the bathwater and sprinkles in some bubbles, and I, of course, can't pee now, you know? Then she proceeds to take off her clothes. I mean, I'm going into hyperventilation here. I was shocked, I was intrigued, I was turned on. And I really had to pee. But it just didn't seem the appropriate thing to do when the object of your fantasies and your adoration is blithely taking off her clothes, throwing in the bubbles. Then she gets in, and there she is, all nice and pink and rosy, with her breasts playing peekaboo with the bubbles. I knew I had to get out of there before she got out, or who knows what I would have done? So I did.

Susan: How long had you been attracted to her by this time?

Lucy: About two years. I was just patiently waiting, and reading, and trying to figure out what this was all about. I still hadn't found any black women to talk to, and not very many people whom I knew were identified lesbians.

After I got the hang of that bathroom stuff, I locked the door. I mean, a woman can only take so much when she's in the throes of deep passion. I beamed sexual thoughts her way, I fantasized joining her in the bathtub . . .

Susan: What were you going to do?

Lucy: I was going to kiss those lovely little tits that kept peeking at me through the bubbles, that for sure. I never got much lower than that in my mind.

I just didn't know where to start. Books are great, but

were not practical for telling me how to sit down with a woman and say, "Jeez, I'd like to fuck your brains out."

It turns out she was starting to be attracted to me. Only she was worried because I was this young black girl.

Susan: How old were you?

Lucy: I was twenty-three and she was thirty. One evening she came and sat on my bed and we had this weird conversation. She was saying things like how she didn't want to exploit me, and how she really cared about me as a friend, and all this wordy shit. I was very perplexed. Besides, I was also very distracted, because she had on only (I checked) this sweet little T-shirt thing, very V-necked, and she was leaning over, wanting to have this heart-to-heart chat.

Then we moved to another house, and by this time I know she's attracted, and she's figured out she's attracted, and we do this little dance. We sit together on the couch and watch television and hold hands. But we are only good friends. Or we give each other back rubs every night because we work all day at such stressful jobs. I think we manufactured crises so we could get back rubs from each other. But we were only friends. It was during this period that I got to know the power of denial. But I knew we were getting a lot touchier and feelier than just good friends, no matter what all those other feminists or other lesbians were doing, helping each other love their bodies and going on those weekends with a speculum, looking at each other's cervix.

Then one time we went camping together in Rocky Mountain National Park. We're in a tent, and it's really cold, so Dana said I should come over and snuggle next to her. She put her arms around me, and we snuggled, and I remember her whispering, just before I fell asleep, "I really love you." I woke up! I was thinking, this sounds promising, so I say, "What did that mean?" And she says, "Nothing, go to sleep." And then I was mad. But I didn't know what to do, so I went to sleep.

Then on the way home we had this intense conversation, and I said, "I love you too," and she drove into this big mud slide. I was furious. We had to dig ourselves out. Then I said, "We're not going to avoid this topic." She said, "Yes, we are. Have you ever played Botticelli?" And we drove all the way home playing this game, which I'd never played before, but I was very mad and very good at it and beat her all the way home.

Then we decided to lay carpet. I was always laying the corners in closets so I made all these jokes about, "I'd sure like to come out of the closet." She said, "Bye now, I've got to go to work." Then she came home and said, "You know, coming out of the closet generally means that you want to become a lesbian," at which point I said, "I didn't know it meant that." And I went to bed. *She* was furious [laughter].

Anyway, the back rubs were getting to be too much, and the tension was getting higher, and one evening I wrote her a letter about how I felt and gave it to her. She came up to my bedroom the next morning, sat on the edge of the bed, read the letter again, and said, "I could have written this." Then she was really quiet. I said, "So, what? What are you thinking about?" And finally she says, "I'm thinking about how to make a pass at you."

Susan: Did you become lovers that morning?

Lucy: Yes. She kissed me right here [Lucy points to her cheek] and I kissed her right there [she points to her other cheek], and our lips traveled slowly until they met. It was wonderful. I, of course, had to go for her breasts; I'd been fantasizing about them for three years, now I had to touch them. It was just as wonderful as I thought, and

I had an orgasm right then and there. You know, the objects of my affection were just right there, mine for the touching.

Then neither of us knew what to do because neither of us had ever made love with a woman before. Dana says, "Let's snuggle, we both know how to do that." We chatted, and things got a little bit easier, and then we were able to make love.

Susan: When you think about making love with Dana, what are some of your favorite scenes?

Lucy: God, back then we did it all the time. We were never out of bed, for like two and a half years. Then we thought, there must be a life out there that we're missing.

Among my favorite times were when we tried every position in the *Loving Women* book. Some of them were very complicated. It was fun.

Susan: Do you remember a complicated one that you could . . . ?

Lucy: The scissors maneuver. We would be snuggling, naked, freshly bathed, candles lit, incense burning, phone turned off, dogs put out, door locked. Then we would look at the picture and get in position, in the case of the scissors maneuver, both lying on our sides with our legs intertwined so you can, in theory, rub clits together. I would read the instructions out loud, "It says raise the left leg and slide down. Oh god, you're too heavy!" We'd try her leg on the bottom, my leg on the bottom, her twisted this way, me twisted that way. We would pause to look at the picture to see if this was really what they meant. Then we would try to figure out how to move. We discovered that the one person can't really move because her leg is stuck on the bottom so we figured out that that person has to stay still, while the person who is perpendicular, so to speak, can move.

But then, what are you going to do with the foot that is in your face? Trust me, we tried this. If you hold on to it, the person can't move. And if you don't, then they are always hitting you in the face with it. I would say, "I just could never get the hang of fucking your big toe. Maybe if you painted it with toenail polish." Then I'd start rubbing her foot and say, "Where'd they say that G-spot was?" And she'd say, "It's right between the big toe and the next one, I saw it in a chart once." And then we'd burst into hysterical giggles. All the other positions weren't bad, but that one was just too much. We figured out that you had to be very young and very thin and very athletic in order to pull it off.

Susan: What else did you try?

Lucy: I had read about vibrators by then, this whole scenario where you do the vibrator all over her body. So here we are in the throes of passion, we're touching everything we could possibly touch, I get out the vibrator and am going to rub it gently over her breasts and on down until I reach her clitoris, and then drive her crazy. Well, I put it on her chest, and she jumps three feet, "What are you doing?" So that killed everything. "Where do you read this stuff?" she says, "It feels like you're trying to defibrillate my heart." She was working in a hospital at the time.

We went through this period of time experimenting with different things. We never could get the hang of those Ben-Wa balls, you know, those two steel balls you stick in your vagina? To me, it just feels like two steel balls in my vagina. All it does is force you to practice your vaginal muscle exercises, because you don't want anybody to see steel balls dropping out while you walk.

We tried one of those double-sided dildos. It was very technical, each person getting it inserted into her vagina, and then trying to figure out how to move so it doesn't come out. That got to be pretty fun, like, "Hold it, stop, it slid out!" Then we got a bladder infection from using it, so that had to go.

I didn't want my friends to know I had one of those, because if you're a lesbian, theoretically, you don't want to mess with penises, right? I, of course, have always liked penises, so it didn't bother me too much. But keeping it concealed was a problem; it's not something you can keep tucked away in your underwear drawer and explain that it is a muscle relaxer. Or a stress releaser.

We each got our own vibrators because I need more stimulation than Dana does. She has what I call a little peashooter, barely enough motion or noise to turn on an ant. I have a slightly bigger version that she says has a motorcycle engine. Hers goes "hmmm"; mine is ".HMMM."

At this point we are startled by a knock on the door. Lucy's supper has arrived, steaming hot and smelling delicious. She eats the hush puppies, but the barbecued ribs and baked beans gradually cool and congeal on the plate, our discussion more interesting than food.

Susan: What are some other special sexual times that you remember?

Lucy: One of my favorite memories is when Dana had long hair, and she started at my head and waved her hair all the way down my body, really soft touching all over. And she did oral sex on me, and I remember thinking, Wow, she must really love me. Because somewhere in the back of my mind I used to think oral sex was wrong or dirty or perverted. And that she was willing to do that, I thought, was really fantastic. And that's when I realized that probably this was a permanent commitment, that it was going to be long-term. Now don't ask me why I equated going down on someone with long-term commitment, but that's what it always signified in my brain, Wow, she may as well propose marriage or something. We giggle about that now, but it still ranks up there; it's a special thing for her too.

Another favorite time we were just outside the park again. It was a real cold winter night, we had wine, it was our anniversary. Dana had planned this real seduction scene. We got the wood stove all stoked up, and she read the Rose of Sharon section from the Song of Solomon in the Bible. You have to use your imagination a bit and change the pronouns, but I didn't know the Bible could be so pornographic. It was quite moving, actually, quite erotic. It was warm, and we could be together, we had a lot of time to make love. She would pour wine over my breast and lick it off, which was one of my personal favorites. It was a wonderful time.

Susan: What do you think the importance of those early sexual times is to a relationship that is going to continue for a long time?

Lucy: I think that real intense sexual time helped set a lot of our communication patterns, like talking in bed at night before we go to sleep. And talking again in the morning before we leave for work. Making a commitment not to go to sleep angry at each other, which is a lot easier to keep early in the relationship than later on. Being there for each other. Of course, we already had a friendship established before we were lovers. We knew each other well.

Susan: What do you think is the relationship between being sexual and being intimate?

Lucy: Intimacy is being close and talking and sharing ideas and plans and really communicating. For me, I can't have really good sex unless I have intimacy. Because sex starts in my head. I have to feel intimate and feel like I know and trust the person before I can be sexual with them.

Susan: Do you like to talk while you're making love?

Lucy: I do. I talk a lot and Dana giggles, which really turns me on, because it's fun to make her laugh, and to say really shocking, outrageous things, and . . .

Lucy: Well, it's kind of embarrassing.

Susan: Would you tell me anyway?

Lucy: Well, there are a lot of stories . . .

Susan: You can close your eyes, and I won't look at you.

Lucy: I'm already not looking at you, you notice that!

Susan: So, set the scene, where are you?

Lucy: We are in bed, and she has something she is reading, something totally nonfiction. She's propped up on her pillow, her glasses are on, the light's on. I'll get in bed and am real quiet for a minute, then I turn to her and say, "I had this fantasy today." And she says, "Not while I'm reading. I really want to finish this book." I say, "Okay." Then I roll over to her and start whispering real soft that I had this fantasy that . . . I can't do this . . . [she takes a deep breath] I say, "We're on an airplane, and it's night, they've dimmed the cabin lights, and we're both snuggled under a blanket. I pretend that I am sleeping on your shoulder, but do you know what I'm really doing? I'm slowly sliding my hands under your skirt, your skirt is going up and my hands are going up, but nobody notices, because we're both covered up with a blanket." At which point she says, "The same blanket?" "No, no," I say, "two separate blankets, so they don't get suspicious. And my hand is slowly going up your leg, ever so slowly, and you're asleep. My hand is going up really slowly, and I come to the edge of your underwear." She's still trying to read her book, but I'm starting to actually do what I'm talking about, my hand sliding under her nightgown. She has this little curl in her pubic hair — she'd die if she knew I was telling you this — and I start playing with her curl and talking, "I slowly start playing with your curl. My fingers slide lower and lower and lower." By this time I have her attention. "My hand is sliding lower and I play with your curl, I touch your dewy, sweet clit, I just twirl it around, it's so soft, and it's so smooth and it's so round."

around, it's so soft, and it's so smooth and it's so round."
And then she starts to squirm, and I continue, "I just keep
rubbing and rubbing until you wake up. And then I keep
rubbing and whispering in your ear how much I love you,
and how much I want to fuck your brains out, right here
on this airplane before we land. And how I'm going to
ease off your underwear so my hand can find you better."
Then she starts moaning, and I say, "You are going to
want to moan, but we have to do this totally silently
because we don't want the people in front or behind us to
notice. You can move up and down, but you can't move
too much. And you can't make any noise, you've got to be
quiet." So I'm doing this and I'm telling her about it, and
pretty soon she's very interested in what I'm talking about,
the book has closed, the glasses are off, the light is out,
and we get down to business. Afterward she says, "You
ought to write these stories down. Nobody would believe
this prim, proper middle-class black woman could talk so
dirty." She likes that one, the airline story one.

Dana likes to call it making love, as opposed to having
sex or fucking. But I can't say, with a straight face,
"Would you like to make love?" I just can't. I giggle the
whole time. Suppose we're sitting at the kitchen table,
doing our finances, I look into her eyes and say, "Let's go
fuck." I could never have said, "Shall we go and make
love?" It just wouldn't have come out right. Besides, it
wouldn't have the shock value.

So I'm very vocal during sex, I whisper a lot, and talk
a lot and encourage her. I'm very descriptive, my fingers
are always matching what I'm saying, and it drives her
crazy. I've described things in such intimate detail Dana
says she can never look at her breasts now without seeing
those perky pink tits that winked at me in the bubbles of
the bubble bath.

Susan: Do you think up these scenes during the day,
or are they just impromptu?

Lucy: I think about them during the day, staring at my computer screen, while I'm supposed to be writing a grant. Sometimes I call her up at work, she picks up the phone, I say, "I'm going to fuck your brains out when we get home, so be ready." Or I'll say, "I'll meet you at home in fifteen minutes," which drives her crazy, especially if she can't come home. "I'll meet you at home in fifteen minutes, and I'm going to rip off your clothes and throw you down on the couch, and I'm going to eat your pussy. That's what I'm having for lunch."

Sometimes she gets mad, "Shhh," she says, "I'm not alone in the office," which instantly inspires me to new and greater heights. "They don't know I'm talking about pulling off your underwear," and so on. She blushes and giggles and says, "I told you, don't do that! I can't leave the office right now, so I'm going to go around wet all afternoon." She cracks me up. Here we've been together nearly twenty years and she's still blushing and giggling.

So then she says, "You're too wicked. Don't ever call me at work again and whisper to me like that." But she doesn't hang up on me, of course.

Susan: How often do you have sex together?

Lucy: Not as often as we'd like. About once a week, Sunday nights. If a friend calls and asks can they drop by, I say, "No, I'm going to take Dana to bed and have serious sex." Dana says, "Who are you telling that to?" and I say, "Your mother." Of course I'd only say that to our closest friends, but she's never sure. She says, "I never know about you."

Susan: Do you talk about sex with your friends?

Lucy: Sometimes our friends get stuck. They say, "God, we haven't had sex in months." So I say, "Well, what are you doing about it?" And they are all perplexed, "What do you mean, what are we doing about it?" I say, "Well, can you make an appointment to have sex? Can you have a date? You could have a bed picnic." And then they say,

"What's a bed picnic?" and I tell them and they're intrigued. I try to suggest different things they can do to spark things up. I really encourage them to take time. If they can't remember how they used to do it, they can read each other a story. If they are cuddled down and nice and clean and relaxed and read a good story, and nothing ignites after that, then they need to go to therapy.

Susan: What's one of your favorite stories?

Lucy: Tee Corrine writes some nice ones. And there's this one scene in Kathleen Fleming's *Lovers in the Present Afternoon* about a couple in a thunderstorm that is to die for. And there are some good videos, although I always want to see how the story line develops. "Lucy," Dana says to me, "there is no story line." She gets turned on and wants to do business right then and there, but I want to discuss the characters. "You're impossible," she says. "Nobody does character assessment of erotic videos." "Well, I do," I say.

Susan: What's a bed picnic?

Lucy: It's a New Year's Eve tradition that Dana and I have, although you can do one any time. We go to the store and buy things like shrimp and strawberries and some grapes and really nice-looking oranges. And sparkling cider, maybe cheese and French bread. We take a bath and have clean sheets, and candles all around. We get in bed naked. Then we usually talk, we're very big on talking. Like on New Year's Eve we talk about what kinds of things we feel good about from the year that's past, and how we think we did as a couple, and what kinds of things we'd like to do for the next year. We just snuggle and talk, and then we feed each other. An orange is very sexy, because you can each eat half and kiss. And then you get to lick all the juice off her lips and wherever else it falls.

We've been together nineteen years now, and people

say to us, "Do you still like sex?" Yes! And we'd like it more often if we could get it and weren't too tired.

Susan: Has it taken an effort to still be so sexual with each other, or is it just natural for you both?

Lucy: We had to work on it. Sometimes I put little notes in her purse, or in her appointment book, or I'll drive by her car at work and put a note on her steering wheel, so when she opens the door there's this note describing what I'd like to do to her: "Tonight you have an appointment with a lovely and alluring stranger. She will appear at your bedroom door. She will be naked. She will be oily. She will massage your neck and your back and your arms. She will lovingly rub your buns. [That really turns her on.] Then she will turn you over and start from your feet and rub up, until she gets to your temple of joy. Then . . ." Then I stop the note and put three little dots. That drives her crazy.

But all this takes effort, to compose a seductive Post-it note, to drive out of your way, get out of the car, stick it in, lock her door. To stop what you are doing in the middle of the day and phone up with some outrageous suggestion. Yeah, we work at it. But it's important.

I'm working on a new scene right now. You know how airplanes sort of thrust or surge as they start their descent? In this scene Dana comes just as she feels that surge. Or, she comes just as her ears pop from the change in cabin pressure. What a combination that must be. I'm working on it, and will try it out soon. It'll drive her crazy!

Amy

"Sexual satisfaction in an intimate
relationship fills you up."

I never felt sexual toward women. I felt close emotionally, but I couldn't figure out how sex was going to be
any different than with men, you know, sort of an act.
When I was twenty-three a lesbian friend introduced me to
a bunch of her friends, and there was this one woman that
was very attractive, dark hair, big, gorgeous green eyes. We
ended up driving around all night, and I thought, now
wouldn't this be an interesting experience. It was mostly
an intellectual thing, why don't I just try this?
There we were, kind of flirting around each other.

Finally I said, "Look, either I'm going to stay here with you, or I'm going to leave right now." She said, "Come on, you're staying." And, even though she was my first woman lover, I felt oddly capable. I thought, I'm going to do to her what I think would feel good to me.

Amy and I are talking upstairs in the house she shares with Julia, her partner of less than a year. To ensure some privacy from much coming and going downstairs, we have moved from the living room to their large bedroom and are sitting across from each other on brocade chairs, an end table between us holding teacups and a plate of chocolate chip cookies. Around us are piled boxes, some still taped shut, others open and spilling their contents, evidence of Amy and Julia's recent merging of all their belongings.

Amy is a thirty-eight-year-old Jewish woman with black hair, bright dark eyes, dark eyebrows, and clear skin, coloring so striking she lights up the space around her. She is wearing black slacks, a bright turquoise blouse, and matching silver-and-turquoise necklace and earrings. She speaks rapidly and with ease, gesturing all the while.

Amy: I was raised in a family that was very open about nudity. We all knew each other's bodies, including my two older brothers, my sister, and me. It was not a big deal. And there was never any hiding of the facts: this is what a man does, this is what a woman does, this is your clitoris. Everything was anatomically correct.

Susan: How did you feel about it?

Amy: I don't remember feeling any way about it. It was just something to be understood. A lot of things that went on in my family were very intellectual. You understand it, therefore it is. In my mind, if I made things intellectual, it was fine to explore.

As a little girl, I remember seeing my brothers with erections and being puzzled, wondering, where is that going to go inside of me or anybody else? But then I thought, oh well, my brothers are gross anyways, you know, burpers and farters, and probably they aren't going to find a place for that to go.

I think my mother was intrigued by gay men, and she would sometimes identify that two men were together by using the Yiddish word *fagala*. It was sort of safe to talk about if it wasn't in English.

There was, of course, an assumption that you fall in love and get married and have children. That was something taken for granted. One day when I was seventeen I came home, and my mother and father were sitting together on a chair, kind of snuggling. My mother says, "I know you run in a pack of friends. Are you seeing anyone in particular?" "Mom!" I said, "no!" And she said, "I'm just asking. Don't hang on to it forever." I was shocked, hearing my mother say I didn't need to be a virgin forever. My father was shocked too. "Margie!" he said. And she replied, "Well? We didn't, so? Why should she?"

Susan: Did you have relationships with boys? With girls?

Amy: I remember I didn't date much, but I had crushes on boys. I wanted to have some kind of physical relationship with them, dating and kissing and that stuff. There wasn't much of an emotional connection, though. I always had emotional connections with my girlfriends, but not sexual feelings.

My first sexual experience with a boy was when I was thirteen or so, and I remember thinking, This is odd, having someone's hands on my body. He felt in my vaginal area, and I thought, Am I supposed to think that this is feeling really good? Because it doesn't. The idea of it turned me on, but actually, it didn't do anything for me. I was glad I'd had the experience, though, because I'd heard about it, and, I thought, maybe it will get better later on.

I would mess around with my younger brother too, when I was ten maybe, and he was fourteen. We were never unclothed, just kind of feeling around each other. One time he was on my back, kind of getting himself off on me. We had a talk about it, and I said, "I don't want to go any further with this, this isn't comfortable." So we stopped. It was interesting, though, and again the idea of it was kind of a sexual turn-on, but in actuality, it wasn't. I didn't want to do that with my brother; he was ultimately gross and ucky.

Susan: Were you ever sexual with men?

Amy: Yes, my first intercourse came when I was eighteen or nineteen. I had actually come here to Montana, very far away from home, and met this guy. He was in his mid to late thirties, kind of off-the-wall, charming, wonderful. He was very sexy in what he was saying to me, but I felt safe with him. I thought, here's a guy who knows stuff, and who thinks I'm great. So I went to him one day and said, "I've never made love with anybody before, would you like to make love with me?" He said, "Oh, I'd be honored."

What a delightful guy. He was slow and patient and would describe to me what feels good to men. But intercourse hurt very much, and I bled a lot. And I wasn't interested in having a long-term thing. He, of course, wanted to do this over and over and over again.

After that I had a couple of other boyfriends here and there, but nothing that was serious or lasted long. I never quite enjoyed penetration from a penis, although I liked the idea of thinking about how excited we all got. But then there wasn't much culmination for me from intercourse itself. Clitoral stimulation was different, but the guys I was with really didn't know what to do. I thought, well, this is disappointing.

I think a lot, though, about the things that make men excited, the things that could make an erection. Erections fascinated me, and still do. I don't know why, but I find them very stimulating. There's something about the visual excitement and release.

Susan: Tell me some more about your first woman lover.

Amy: It was a very heady kind of thing. I was twenty-three at the time, and sex with women didn't become more emotional for me until many years later, when I was more available to open up emotionally.

I remember I was interested in what she wanted to do with me, in what turned her on. She would lick my breasts, and I remember thinking, Does that feel good to her? Because it's okay for me, but no big deal. I remember asking her, What feels good to you? And everything felt good to her. So I thought, This is all a learning experience, because not everything feels all that great to me.

Everybody has a different body flavor, and I remember not liking how she tasted very much. But I thought, Well, I'm just experimenting anyway, I can live through this. I haven't had many lovers, but the ones I have had, how they taste is a very big deal with me. All my senses are heightened, and I didn't want to lick my lovers if I didn't like how they tasted. I would just withdraw from licking them and do something else.

I liked the configuration of body to body with that first woman lover, and I liked being inside her with my hands. I liked that a lot. But I don't remember any emotional connection. I remember being with a woman was more intriguing to me than being with a man. Women are more interesting sexually to me than men are. Men are very obvious. They get erect, they ejaculate, finito, done. Women you have to figure out, things are not as overt, there are different degrees of what feels good, different climaxes, all kinds of things go on.

My first woman pretty much tried everything, but wasn't a very good lover to me. I don't know whether it was me not being able to relax, but I don't think she was particularly sexy or smooth. She didn't draw me out at all. We had fun, she was sweet and fun. But I knew I wasn't going to be with her for a very long time. She wasn't complicated enough for me.

Susan: What about your experiences with other women?

Amy: A woman making love to me had never been enough to fill me up and get me to climax. I always wanted to fantasize about something. With another woman lover, someone I saw when I first moved here, I learned that fantasies could be about us, too. This woman was very sexy, very uninhibited, very sensual, a wonderful lover. And she just kind of took me by surprise. I was so drawn to that sexual connection that I found I was paying attention to where I was. I was actually present. I had never really had that before. I realized that I could tap into my own desire as a means of turning myself on. I could let myself just let her make me feel good, instead of thinking my way to orgasm.

I had two lovers who could vaginally ejaculate, totally wet the bed. You feel this drench of liquid on your hands. God, it's a wonderful feeling of satisfaction to bring another woman to orgasm this way. I'm not capable of this, at least so far. Maybe I am and just haven't tapped into it, who knows?

Susan: You said earlier that you only gradually became emotionally open to women. What do you think happened over the years to make this possible?

Amy: I think my own comfort with being with women

improved, my own belief that it was actually okay. I think earlier on I was spellbound by the idea of being with women and the experience of actually being with women. But I was also very confused and closeted about what actually made me feel good, and how much of that I would expose to the people close to me. That conflict was there for years, and still is to some degree. I have my own homophobia.

Susan: Can you say more about that conflict?

Amy: The conflict was, Here are all these feelings for women, and this is what feels best to me, but can I actually open myself to that, given that this is not going to go over well in my family? To some degree I kept thinking, maybe it *is* a phase, and until the right person comes along, I'm not going to rule out that that right person isn't going to be a man. Up until just a year and a half or two years ago I would have sex once every few years with a trusted male friend, just to check in, to remind myself that even though I love this guy, and even though he has always wanted to marry me, it doesn't fill me up the way that making love with a woman does, and did, and always has.

It would be much easier to get married, to have children, to raise our kids Jewish, to instill a sense of cultural history and tradition. But if I were to marry a man, even as close as I feel to this man friend, it wouldn't be fair to him. Because I would always be wondering and looking around at women and attracted to women.

It's interesting that my first sexual experience with a woman was right after my mother died. I don't think I could have been with women while my mother was alive. I must have felt that there would be some disappointment for my mother, that her daughter would be a lesbian. I've always held my parents in such high esteem, and their opinions have always been very important. I've always tried to please them, to be a good kid and a smart kid and all of that, sometimes to a sicko degree. But after my mother died, there was some freedom to explore.

I remember coming out to my father. I knew if I made it intellectual, rather than an emotional issue, it would be something we could talk about. So I said, "I'd like to discuss with you the difficulties and joys of having an alternative lifestyle. And what it means to me." It was a very interesting discussion, and he was very supportive. He said, "As a parent, you don't want your kid to do anything that would make life more difficult. And you've chosen a path that is more difficult." I said, "Dad, if I could choose, I would not choose this. But here it is."

I think if I had the connection with men that I have with women, I would be straight. I would love my women friends, but I would have a husband. If there was that sense of intrigue with men, that whatever it is that spins you around to make the sex be good, then that's where the connection would be. And that would be really nice, but that's not me. That's some fantasy of what I thought would be really nice. What is actually really nice is being with Julia.

Susan: Can you tell me what attracted you to Julia?

Amy: When I first met Julia she was very open, kind of snappy and fun, a quick wit. And she's great looking, incredibly great bone structure, a square jaw, high cheekbones, beautiful blue eyes. A beautiful mouth, great teeth, these gorgeous dimples. I think she's classically beautiful. So the outside package is nice. And there's this little glint that she has that's very fun. And a style that is equally playful and inviting, but protective.

We became involved sexually very quickly, which is not my style or hers either. I wonder, you know, how you can feel so close to somebody when you haven't had the time to experience getting close. I remember the first time we made love, if I was resistant to anything, if I pulled back, that wasn't okay with her, she would push me a little bit, she would encourage me to experience it as whatever it was, and not to shy away so quickly.

Susan: What was she doing?

Amy: My body is very sensitive, and she was pinching my nipples, or sucking them in a hard way. Then she would check in with me with her eyes. It was a little bit painful. I watched her reaction, and she was quite enjoying this. I thought, Well, I can live through this, and maybe it will lead me to something else.

It turns me on that she knows what she's doing and takes control, because I have always pretty much been the one in control. I would take control as a protective means, you know. Nothing was going to hurt me, or get in there. Julia had this confident way of saying, "Amy, don't get all fidgety here. Just experience it." And I would. There was a different level of trust. It was Julia that really encouraged me to open up to vaginal penetration. She could tell when I was letting go, and when I was tight, and she would just stop, and gently say, "Let go." And god, I would melt. I don't know whether to call it intrigue or some glint of excitement that she has, or just that she's so damned sexy and it's directed at me and with me. But, hell yes, I'm going to try this with her.

I now have a sense of growing sexually, that I have come to a place where I can trust my partner, where I can give my body over and experience different things, things like vaginal penetration, that would hurt before. But because I'm relaxing into them, they don't hurt. Before I would be wet, but all tight and not trusting. I've never experienced a vaginal orgasm, my orgasms have always been clitoral, but now I am wondering, am I getting more open to maybe a vaginal orgasm?

It's very interesting to make love and do some different things, although initially I'm very resistant. It might be fun to play with some toys, like dildos, but, oh god, when

I think about it, I just embarrass myself. It's intriguing but embarrassing to me somehow. I think I'll ultimately try, and see where it goes, if I can stop laughing about it. You know, some purple dildo [she chuckles]. It just seems so ridiculous. [She pauses.] This is the first time I've ever looked for a long-term relationship, and I think that is reflected in the sex.

Susan: How so?

Amy: When you're first getting together, you don't know the other person very well, except in a tactile, physical sense. Over time, as you invest more emotionally, as I've invested more emotionally, I've become more emotional in my lovemaking. Because I've fallen in love. I wasn't in love before. Now it's okay to be emotional, it's okay to be vulnerable. And it shows in our lovemaking. I tear up, in a joyous way. I don't feel much in control. I'm more willing to be open, to experiment. Whatever we do, hurt or not, I can tell her. There's more of a sense of, why not try this? It opens a whole new range of possibilities of things to explore. It's been about a year, and I think we've really just begun to tap into all the different things we can do with each other.

Susan: Like what do you want to do, or especially enjoy doing?

Amy: There are times when each of us speaks of wanting to have a penis, to be inside the other one. That's a turn-on and an exposure and is fascinating to me. Even though it's a very delicate subject within the lesbian community. And one that I don't particularly want to broach. But there's something wonderful about being able to talk to a partner about it.

And I love it when she's lying on my back and rubbing herself against my tailbone, which meets right up with her clit. I like feeling her weight on me. We're very hot, and the sweat creates a slick between us, lubricating all of our skin. It's very exciting to me. It's easy to create pictures of her, as if I'm floating up above and watching.

Her clit is set higher than mine, so she can get stimulation from rubbing body to body, whether she's on my back or facing me, rubbing against my pubic bone. Whereas I'm wrapped underneath; it's just the way I'm built. We're all built very differently.

I've never thought of myself as being very good at oral sex. I like the way Julia tastes, but I feel fairly incompetent with my mouth, just because I've not practiced much. She says I do just fine. I feel very competent with my hands, and the rest of my body.

I'm now curious about how we can work out a mutual orgasm. It's tough. You hear about couples that can, and I'm thinking, how? How do they do this? And wouldn't it be nice?

Julia and I have talked about it. She says, "There's lots of ways. We'll work on it." Then I get frustrated, because we're having to become gymnasts to try and get this elusive mutual orgasm.

Susan: How are you trying to do it?

Amy: By interlocking our legs to where we can rub clit on clit, but it doesn't get me right.

Susan: There're mouths. You can do a sixty-nine position and both do mouths simultaneously.

Amy: I've never been able to have an orgasm that way because I could never concentrate. There's too much going on. And I like to make love with my eyes open, and look at my lover, and talk to my lover. And really be with her.

Susan: How often do you make love?

Amy: A couple of times a week. But we are very sexual all the time, even when we're not bringing each other to orgasm. We kiss and hug and snug and touch all the time. We banter with each other, titillate each other, all the time. So when we do actually make love, it's wonderful, but I don't feel like we're missing anything when we don't for a few days. Or a week. I feel comfortable saying, "I'm absolutely attracted to you, I desire you totally, I'd die for you . . . and I'm falling asleep."

Susan: Does how much you weigh affect how sexual you feel, or not? [I have noticed a picture across the room of a somewhat heavier Amy.]

Amy: I think it has. I used to be very heavy, probably sixty or seventy pounds more than I weigh now. I know I was really loved by women when I was that weight, and that was amazing to me because I have a strong sense of what is attractive, and heavy was never attractive to me. But it didn't matter to them; they just loved me. It was my issue.

Once I lost weight, though, I felt more attractive to myself, and I was much more sexually open. I think I had more of a sense of personal power.

Susan: What do you think the importance of being sexual is when you think of it in the context of the rest of your life?

Amy: That's an interesting question. Being sexual builds intimacy, and being sexual makes us a strong unit, gives us a foundation to take out to the rest of the world. I think sexual satisfaction in an intimate relationship fills you up in such a way that nothing else can compare. Being sexual, knowing that I have that closeness with my partner, lends so much to me, to my inner self; it can bring tears to my eyes.

I also strive to keep myself interesting so that I can bring to my partner a person who grows and changes, who doesn't become stagnant. Because if our lives weren't interesting, sex wouldn't be interesting. We need to keep ourselves passionate about what we do and how we care for ourselves and for other people, we need to have interesting lives independently, so we can bring them home to each other. That will then be reflected in our sex lives.

When intrigue continues over a long-term relationship, there are surprises that make you want to be closer and know and learn more about that person. There are sides to all of us that come out over time, kind of a time release effect. I hadn't expected this, to get to see the evolution of somebody.

Susan: Perhaps some of the intrigue is because you have a chance to explore yourself, to experience yourself evolving. Perhaps the "somebody" is you, as well as Julia.

Amy: I think it's all about ourselves. Our lovers are mirrors. If you can find a safe place to experience things, to bounce them off another person, you get to see more parts of yourself. Realistically, all of it is about ourselves.

Grace

"I think being sexual is holy."

I have called myself a homosexual from the time I was ten years old. I had this incredible crush on my fifth-grade history teacher, Miss Thomas. I wrote her letters, which I would put on her car, a blue Chevy Nova, Vermont License Plate Z56989, parking space number 5.

I would go to school early so I could watch her park in her space and walk into the building. After school I would climb a tree right near the teachers parking lot so I could watch her walk out of the building, get into her car, and leave. I did this in all seasons, and it never occurred to me

133

that during the winter, when there were no leaves on the tree, she could see me. But she never let on.

I didn't know what it was that I felt for Miss Thomas, but I knew it was something very different than I had felt with anybody, ever. One day I figured I would look for the answer. I got on my bike — it was crisp and cool, October in New England — and I rode first to my family's Catholic church. I looked at all the literature on the table in the back, but didn't find the answer. Then I went to the next church, a Congregational church, and didn't find it, and to the next one, an Episcopal church, and it wasn't there either.

Then I went to the Unitarian church. There was a pamphlet titled "Love." So I picked that up, and read it, sitting on the church stairs. It talked about different kinds of love and said that sometimes girls and women love each other, that this is homosexual love, and that it's fine. I was really excited and happy, because now I had a word for it: "I'm a homosexual, and this is love I am feeling, and it's fine." So I went to school and told everybody I was a homosexual.

Grace is a slim, thirty-six-year-old woman, with short almost-white blonde hair and glasses. We are sitting at the kitchen table in the Minnesota home she shares with her partner, Lindy. Outside the January night is clear and just zero degrees; ice crystals drift through the air. But inside we are warm and protected, nursing cups of tea. Grace strokes the cat sitting on her lap. Her Border collie sits alertly at her feet.

Grace is a college teacher, an intelligent, thoughtful person who pauses often during the interview, pondering what the best, most honest answers to my questions would be. The second night we talk she produces a large scrapbook and boxes of memorabilia. She has kept everything from the early years of her lesbian life.

Grace: I can document my lesbianism back to the age of ten. When I put my life all together like this I see I had some lesbian identity from the time I was very young. [She sorts through the materials in her memory box, and comes up with a stack of precious letters.]

I wrote Miss Thomas letters, rewrote them, sent her the perfect version, and kept the originals myself. This one is letter number 9, dated March 27, 1970. I was eleven years old. "Miss Thomas. Oh, Miss Thomas how I feel like kissing you. It's just so awful cause I know I never will be able to. But the next best thing for me to do is to be just as good as I can on the track team and get an *A* in history. But, oh Miss Thomas, I love you."

Here's number 15: "Miss Thomas. I just don't know how the heck I'm ever going to stand this summer. I wish they'd shorten the vacation by a month, so I would be able to see you again. Just seeing you is enough for me. Miss Thomas, if it's the last thing I do, I've got to find out your address so I can write to you this summer."

Susan: Did you find out her address?

Grace: Nope . . . nope [she sighs].

Susan: What did Miss Thomas do with your letters?

Grace: I don't know. But she accepted them and never told me to stop writing.

Susan: And how did the kids and the other teachers react?

Grace: Of course everybody at school knew because I told them. In class we'd all have our hands raised to answer a question, and when one of the other kids was called on, instead of answering the question they'd say, "Miss Thomas, Grace loves you." I have my history book in my bookcase there [she gestures into the living room], with notes in it from other kids that say things like, "Good luck with Miss Thomas."

My girlfriends and I would be called "lezzy," so there was definitely some difficulty with it, but I was just right out there, and I did get some support. A couple of teachers talked to me about how I was gonna do during summer vacation, without Miss Thomas.

Unfortunately, Grace's childhood sexual life was not limited to her crushes on teachers.

Grace: I was sexually abused by my father from a very young age. I have a memory as early as four, and it was the worst when I was about seven or eight. The message I got from my Catholic family was that sex was the most beautiful thing in the world, that nobody should touch me between the time I was born and the time I was married, that I should save myself sexually for the man who would be my husband. And while I'm getting this message my father was sexually abusing me. It was a terrifying experience.

Susan: Did that experience impact your sexual life as you got older?

Grace: I'm quite certain that it did, because starting from the time I was twelve I got into drugs and alcohol. And with the drinking and using came a lot of early sexual experiences. I was assaulted by one boyfriend when I was thirteen. And later I would have sex with anybody because I didn't realize I could say no, that I had value.

Like many young lesbians-to-be, Grace had boyfriends as well as girlfriends. Her young sexual life was complicated, confusing, and in many ways painful, but she has pleasant memories as well.

Grace: I had just turned fourteen when a boyfriend kissed me. It was October, really cold and brisk, a bright sky. We'd ridden home together from a theater workshop, and as he got out of the car he just leaned over and gave me the sweetest kiss, just this little brush. It was wonderful, gentle and magical, and really like my first kiss, even though it wasn't.

The first person I actually made love with was a woman, when I was fifteen. Kara and I met at Girl Scout camp, where she was a nineteen-year-old counselor and I was a thirteen-year-old counselor-in-training. We began a very emotionally intense, passionate relationship. We corresponded and visited each other. But I wasn't being sexual with her. We were doing playing kinds of things, where you bump into each other and gaze into each other's eyes forever. We were both infatuated with each other, but weren't doing anything about it.

Susan: Did you kiss?

Grace: No. But endless brushing of hair and back rubs.

Susan: Did it feel erotic?

Grace: It felt ecstatic. I was so happy. I loved it. I remember sitting on her bed and having her brush my hair. I had hair down to the middle of my back, and her brushing it felt very luxurious and warm.

The relationship became sexual when I was fifteen. We used to meet once a month in Boston. By that time I had decided that with my long hair I was attractive to men, so I cut off my hair. I wanted to look like a lesbian.

At the end of one magical day together Kara and I stopped in a beautiful old Episcopal church. We were in some private place in the church, and she leaned up against me, her whole body leaned up against me, and she kissed me. Now that was a kiss! My body just went on fire. We did tongues, hands, everything. It was a big, intense kiss.

The next month when we met we actually made love. I remember the clothes I was wearing, old patched blue jeans, hip huggers you know, faded to perfection, and a red acrylic turtleneck. It was a fabulous outfit. I still have those jeans and that sweater; those were my coming-out clothes.

I don't recall the actual sexual scene as much as I remember the smells later. We had put our fingers inside each other and then we didn't want to wash forever, and I don't think I did! I remember riding the bus back home, keeping myself company by smelling her on my fingers. I was in a separate world where nobody else had ever been. It felt so special. And I felt scared, very scared. Because I was really taking some risks.

Grace's parents suspected that Kara might be a lesbian, and they reacted by threatening their daughter with her life — literally — if the two girls continued to see each other. Grace sustained her relationship with Kara, despite the risks, but during these teenage years she was sexual with boys as well. The summer she was seventeen, she and a boyfriend had a satisfying affair.

Grace: We had this wonderful summer romance. It was very healing and fun. But I was totally confused. Here I was, this diehard lesbian, and I had this boyfriend. And I really loved him.

Susan: Can you compare being in love with Kara and being in love with Sam?

Grace: Well, I was always afraid with Kara, always taking these incredible risks. So there was enormous anxiety associated with being with a woman. And there was an ease about being with Sam. And an approval that I got from my family and from society that, of course, I didn't have when I was with her, when it was secret and I had to hide.

That's part of what really rankles me about being with a man; there's so much privilege associated with it. I feel like when I am with a man I can see through the privilege, and it's so hypocritical.

Susan: What was sex with Sam like for you?

Grace: It was very difficult at first to have sex with him, to allow penetration. I think it had something to do with the sexual abuse, because my mind may have been willing, but my body said, My God, this is scary. So when I could finally have intercourse with him, it was very sweet and very fun. I remember the two of us saying, "Why have we been warned about this?"

Grace's parents eventually discovered that the girls had continued to see each other. They sent Grace to a psychiatrist to be cured and threatened to have her excommunicated from the Church, at a time when, Grace says, "Religion was my mainstay." Her parents said they wouldn't pay college tuition for a homosexual, and they wouldn't let Grace talk to her three younger brothers.

Grace: That was very difficult, very painful. I had the choice of either staying in the family or choosing Kara. And at age sixteen I chose the family. I didn't have any other options, or I didn't think I did.

Instead of going to college Grace worked in Europe for two years, until, as she says, "my parents forgot about my homosexuality." In Europe she had sexual connections with several men, nonsexual romances with several women, and a serviceable sexual involvement with herself.

Grace: I really set out to learn about masturbation when I was in Europe. I had pictures of Kara all over the wall. I would furiously masturbate, and look at her pictures, trying to recreate or sustain that connection we had had. In her room back in the States she had this art poster of rose petals so close up they looked like female genitalia. I would imagine those rose petals and rub really hard on my clit.

There wasn't any finesse or art to what I was doing; it was very utilitarian. I needed to take care of myself.

All this time I was in Europe I knew I was a lesbian, but I was really trying to be straight. I was tortured about this whole confusion. And I was drinking heavily to black out, to check out, to numb out. Most of the times that I had sex with men I did so when I was drunk or nearly so. I had to get really plastered to have sex.

Susan: What would that achieve?

Grace: Well ... [long thoughtful silence] ... I wasn't really making a choice. You know? I didn't have to say, "I am this or I am that." It was just, "I was drunk." But being straight was just so icky that I had to be drunk.

Susan: What was icky about it?

Grace: It just seemed sordid. I had a relationship with an older Italian man who was warm and intelligent and kind of mysterious. But there was nothing emotionally sustaining in my relationships with men. I just longed for a woman.

Susan: Do you think of that longing as being sexual as well as emotional?

Grace: Yeah, because I found that sex with men made me nauseous. And I just wanted breasts! Just the warmth and softness of a woman's body. Of course despite this, I got engaged to the Italian man.

Susan: And how was the sex with him?

Grace: It was really hot. Exciting, different, innovative.

Susan: It didn't make you nauseated?

Grace: It *did* make me nauseous.

He was really strong and insistent. He demanded that I satisfy his needs, like for anal sex, even though he knew that was how I was raped when I was thirteen. So my relationship with him was both wonderful and awful.

But it was helping me to be more clear about being a lesbian. Because the sex stuff with men was for the birds, and the expectations that come with being a woman in relationship to a man, things like you're gonna clean and you're gonna cook and somehow he's more important? Every hair on the back of my neck stands up.

Grace eventually left the Italian man behind, returned home, went to college where — unknown to her parents — she had multiple relationships with women, and a week after graduating, moved to Minnesota.

Grace: I met Sarah the day I moved to Duluth. We moved in together two, maybe three days later, started being sexual that night, and became lovers a week later. We got married after two years and stayed together four years.

She was the one who helped me get sober. She confronted me about my drinking; it was the first time anybody had done that. I have been sober now for the past twelve and a half years.

Susan: How was your sexual life without alcohol?

Grace: It was very hard to have sex sober. All the feelings were new. Alcohol sedates the emotion that's there, so without alcohol I could feel my fear, I could feel my happiness, I could feel my confusion. I could feel what was happening. If my hand was somewhere, I knew it was there. I could feel all the parts of my body. I knew where I started and left off, and where you started. I had never had that experience, knowing the difference between you and me.

And whatever I did sexually, I did consciously. I was really there, you know? I could open my eyes and really see you, see the color of your skin, the color of your eyes, the color of your hair. I knew what time of day it was, I knew who you were. It was very immediate.

Susan: Did you discover erogenous zones that you hadn't had before?

Grace: I discovered nuance of feeling that I hadn't known before. The feeling of building up to an orgasm: I could feel what would happen in my body, where I'd flush, and . . . what I wanted. I could feel what I wanted.

Grace and Lindy have been partners now for four years, but they met seven years ago. At the time Lindy was happily settled in a long-term relationship, but in 1989 her partner, Ruth, was diagnosed with cancer. During the year that Ruth endured treatment and Lindy nursed and supported her, Grace and Lindy were close friends. Ruth died thirteen months later.

Grace: There was an attraction between Lindy and me, but I didn't want to get in a relationship with someone who was intensely grieving somebody else. And if I was going to get into a relationship, I wanted it to last. I wanted it to be on a strong foundation.

It wasn't until ten months after Ruth died that Lindy and I had our first kiss, which is actually a very funny story. Remind me to tell you later. After that first kiss we were kind of nominally sexual for two months. Then she went on a trip, and I started having my incest stuff come up. So all bets between us were off. I plunged into my incest work, and it was over a year before Lindy and I could be sexual again.

During that time we had no kisses, no hand-holding, nothing. We were each other's friends. That was the most important thing. So we have been through a lot together.

We have really been there for each other emotionally, in ways I don't think we could have been if we'd been lovers.

Susan: Why do you say that?

Grace: Being friends made it easier for me to just be there for her, just be her support. Once we became lovers I had expectations that I brought to the relationship that weren't always realistic, that weren't always fair. Like I started feeling jealous of Ruth, and jealous of the attention Lindy spent processing her feelings about Ruth. I felt like her past was a threat.

And because we became lovers Lindy has more of a reaction to my abusive father. If we were just friends she wouldn't feel like she was entitled to tell me what to do. She would just be my support. But as lovers there is pressure from her for me to confront him.

Susan: It's interesting that being lovers seems to give us rights we wouldn't have otherwise.

Grace: Lindy doesn't have a right to tell me how to deal with my father. Nor do I have a right to tell her how to grieve Ruth. As lovers we may want to assume we have rights, but we don't have rights.

Since Grace and Lindy have become lovers, they have been enthusiastic ones. At first they had sex all the time. By now they make love more when they're relaxed and have the time, less when they're pressured by something, but on average perhaps once a week. I asked Grace to describe the last time they made love.

Grace: We were having company in an hour. So we decided we would have a quickie delight, that's what we call it when we don't have much time. We went upstairs, and jumped on the bed and were laughing and jumping on each other. Just playing. Then we got right down to things. We were holding each other real tight, and she sucked on my nipples, and then I sucked on her nipples, and she went down on me and licked me. Then she was laying on top of me, rubbing on me, rubbing our genital areas together. I was pulling on her nipples, and saying I love you, and opening her up from the back, and she came in short order [laughs].

And then right away she started sucking my nipples again. I pulled her over to the side of me and while she was sucking on me and going inside me with her fingers, I made myself come. That was also in very short order. So that was our quickie delight. Then we just laid there together for a little bit, saying I love you.

When I'm coming, I love to just look right into her eyes and say "I love you." It's very nice.

Susan: There's a lot of discussion among lesbians — at least in the literature — about what "having sex" means.

Grace: When I say "have sex" I'm thinking orgasms, and that's both of us, 'cause we usually both have an orgasm.

Susan: What's your favorite thing to have Lindy do to you sexually?

Grace: [Long pause.] So many nice things to think about.

Susan: Okay, your favorite two or three things.

Grace: I just love it when she sucks on my clit. I have great orgasms that way. But I don't get to see her when she's doing that. That's a loss. Another thing I like is for me to be rubbing on my clit, and her going inside me with her finger while her breast is between my legs.

Susan: I'm trying to get a picture of this.

Grace: It's pretty contorted. Another thing I really like is when she's on top of me, rubbing, and I can feel that she's gonna come. I love the changes that happen in her, it makes me very turned on.

And something we've been doing recently that's really fun is, I'll be on top of her, and she'll open her lips and then she opens my lips so our clits are rubbing together.

She likes that, so I like to do that. We're so close I'm kind
of dripping on her, I'm right in her practically.

Susan: Do you make noise when you make love?

Grace: Oh, yeah, you bet. Lots of noise. We talk to
each other a lot. And say what we like and what we want
and describe what we're doing. I like that a lot.

Susan: Is talking a turn-on?

Grace: It's a turn-on, and also I think it makes it real
for me. Because my early experiences of abuse were, this is
not happening. So now by talking out what we're doing, it
makes it real. It's very erotic to be able to say, "This is
what I am doing to you, this is what you are doing to
me." That's really powerful.

I also like what we call "surging." I'll be at work and
boom, there's this surge, that seems to come from my
vagina, and just goes all through me. All of a sudden I
just have this major desire for Lindy. We like to call each
other when we surge, "Honey, I've just surged!"

Susan: So tell me about the first time you kissed.

Grace: It was so funny. We had been friends for the
longest time, and had taken a vacation together. On this
vacation we touched, which produced sexual feelings, but
we didn't do anything genital. And no kissing.

The morning after we came back from our vacation we
were lying in bed together, and we started kissing. It was
the first time we had kissed, and it was, oh my god, she's
a fabulous kisser, she's so wonderful, she's a great kisser.
That's very important so I was really happy and excited.
We'd been in bed some hours, just kissing, when I came
out here to make some coffee. I was wearing the bathrobe
she'd given me for Christmas, had turned the gas on under
the water, and was standing on a chair, trying to get
something out of the cabinet above the stove. Suddenly my
bathrobe went poof, up in flames. "Lindy, what do I
do? . . . I'm on fire!" The robe must have been treated with
something fire retardant, because it didn't burn out of

control, so the experience was just funny. First I was on fire from being with Lindy, and then I was really on fire!

Susan: How important do you think being sexual is to being intimate with Lindy?

Grace: I think it's important that we are lovers, but I don't think it is necessary to be sexual to be intimate. I think that the history of our relationship bears that out because we have been very intimate with each other without being sexual or even sensual. And that was something we both really wanted. We didn't want to have a relationship that was based first on sexualized desire. We first wanted to be friends.

But being lovers adds a fullness, a greater dimension. When we're sexual I feel peaceful. You know, there's a command to a dog, "settle." After we've been sexual I feel settled. I feel touched and reassured and settled at all levels of who I am.

It's not just in bed afterward. I feel confident out in the world. I just love going to work feeling, "You don't know what I do. And what that means to me, and who that makes me." Even though I'm out at work, nobody knows what I do. It's like a secret power source.

So our being sexual does not enhance just our relationship. It enhances my life too. It enhances my sense of self, my sense of who I am in the world.

I think being sexual is holy. It's sacred, it involves a sacred trust. It's this precious gift that we offer. And I want my precious gift to be cherished. And I want to do the same for her.

Being lovers means you're willing to be just bare with the other person. It means being vulnerable. Being myself. It means being real.

Lindy

"Talking about our feelings is our real
bond. Sex is the frosting, not the
main dish."

The more Marcia and I were together, the more fun it
was. Then, on a cross-country drive — a guy I was kind of
involved with was along too — Marcia and I tented
together. And that's when I first was sexually involved
with a woman.

The sleeping bags were on the tent floor, and we just
whipped off our clothes. I've always been attracted to
large-breasted women, and she had quite large breasts,
which were very nice, very nice. I'm sure I started sucking

on her big-time. We didn't have anal sex, but we did everything else, sucking breasts, and sucking everything else, and rubbing everywhere, and hands everywhere. I'm sure I had at least one orgasm, if not two or three.

That was more than twenty years ago — I was eighteen at the time — so it's all kind of a blur in my memory. But it was a powerful first experience. It was such a relief. I felt so free, and so alive, and so real. I felt: This is where I should be.

Lindy is a slim, muscular, energetic woman, now thirty-nine years old. She has agreed to talk with me because I have also talked with her partner, Grace, the subject of the previous profile. By interviewing both women I hope to learn how each partner in a long-term couple contributes to the distinctive sexual culture they are fashioning with each other.

Sitting still for a three-hour interview, however, tests Lindy's patience. She does what she can to stay active, gesturing broadly to accent her words, moving around on her chair, leaning back with spread legs, hands behind her head, leaning forward and tapping on the table. She would much rather be remodeling some corner of the house she and Grace own, or be outside, hiking or skiing.

Lindy did not stay with Marcia, her first love, for the rest of her life, even though commitment to another person is at the heart of Lindy's personality.

Lindy: Maybe it's because I'm a twin, but the minute I'm with somebody I just glom on; I'm going to be with that person the rest of my life.

My mom, with whom I am very close, also instilled the idea of commitment in me. I was in fourth grade, about ten years old, when I had my first kiss, with Bobby Cook. I came home and told my mom, and she said, "It's important to save" — I remember that verb — "to save those kinds of experiences for people you really love." I took that in, because later on I would think, Well, should I be saving this?

Susan: Were you also attracted to girls when you were a youngster?

Lindy: Mary Jones was a cutie! And a hell of a tennis player; I was really into tennis. She was the first female I recognize having an attraction for. I was about thirteen or fourteen years old and did not have a clue as to how to proceed. I remember feeling very frustrated. And angry.

At the same time these boys were continually asking, "You want to go out? Want to go to the prom?" Aargh. Eventually I graduated into boyfriends who were pretty androgynous, and probably bisexual, now that I look back. This would have been the mid-seventies; they were nice, sensitive, long-haired hippie guys. There was a lot of heavy petting, and intercourse a few times, but I always felt like I shouldn't be there. Not because I felt guilty, but it just did not feel like me!

The word "lesbian" was very remote. There were times when I would test it out. I'd say, "Lesbian. I wonder if I'm a lesbian?" And then I'd get really scared that I could be. *Really* scared. So I didn't have any lesbian relationship until Marcia, when I was eighteen.

Then, when Marcia and I did become sexual, I thought, This may be my first relationship with a woman, but it's also, by god, gonna be my last. I didn't see the bias in the world against lesbians. I just thought, This is what I've been missing all this time! I was in my own little bubble.

The reason Marcia, and of course Paul, and I were driving across country was so I could go to college and she could go to seminary. Very soon after our sexual experience, she decided it was wrong. She had the church's stuff coming at her. So she called it off. I was furious at her.

Then in college I got to know this other woman, Amy, and we started a relationship. By the time Amy came around, I knew I was a lesbian. I was really happy and proud and felt so good. And like most of the times in my life when I feel that way, I shared it with my mom. I really respect what my mom says, and I really listen to her, even now.

Well, I told her about Amy and what it meant, and my mother cried for three days. It shocked the hell out of me that she reacted that way. I thought she'd be her amazingly caring, sensitive self. No-o-o. She was devastated. The first thing that came to her mind was that she wouldn't have any grandchildren. It took her a long time to get used to the idea.

Amy was wild. I loved that. She would stay out all night, and we had a great time.

Susan: How about sex. Was she wild about that too?

Lindy: She was pretty good. She was a lot smaller woman, so it wasn't as much fun for me. I like *big* women. But it was nice. Except she was half involved with this guy. And ultimately married him. So that was a bummer.

By that time I needed to get with a woman who knew she was a lesbian. I went back to Minnesota after college, and then I met Ruth. A wonderful, wonderful woman. We met at a camp for kids. It was clear we wanted to be together, so at the end of the season, we went to her cabin near Ely. And made mad, passionate love on the floor the first night!

It was fall. Crisp, and full of color, the leaves were changing. The raspberries coming out, ripe, and we were ripe too! We had suppressed these desires all summer, and once we were free, we just kind of let 'er rip. We were rolling on the floor and tearing each other's clothes off and kissing. We did some big-time licking and big-time sucking and all that stuff.

Ruth was very woman-identified. I thought, if I'm going to devote my life, *again*, to somebody — which I was wont to do — then it seemed like she was okay.

I remember another time, when we'd been together some years, we were skiing — it was the middle of winter, zero degrees — and we decided to make love right there, so we did. We left our ski boots on and our shirts on, but everything else was off. It was cold! So it was fast and furious, but it was really fun.

Ruth was physically very strong, a tall Finlander dyke. So I just felt really good. I was totally gaga. For ten years I was gaga. Then, just six years ago, she was fine one day, and then discovered this discharge. She waited for her next period, but it was still there. We went into Minneapolis, and, even though she had had two normal pap smears earlier, she now had a tumor on her cervix that was already big. It was, whew. We spent a year trying to get rid of it. Surgeries and chemo and radiation, all that stuff. But it was absolutely rapid. Fast. Terrible. Awful. She was diagnosed in January of 1989 and she died February of 1990. So that was a lifelong partnership.

I was proud to be able to be with her, all the time, every day, every minute until the moment she died . . . and beyond.

Then it took me two years, I was pretty much under the covers, depressed, grief-stricken, utterly, utterly awful stuff. I sought out help from a therapist because I knew I needed help. I could not do this one alone. I saw the therapist while Ruth was sick, and then, after Ruth died, I saw her for a long time. It really helped to get back in touch with the world. And so that took forever. Still. It's still ... [she takes a deep breath] you know, it'll always be hard.

Lindy leans back in her chair, drops her head to her chest, and wraps her arms around her head. She stays motionless, holding that position for maybe ten seconds. Then she takes a deep breath ... another one ... removes her arms, lifts her head ... another breath. And continues.

Lindy: After Ruth died I just knew that her body was just a body, and that her spirit was everywhere, and has always been everywhere and will always be everywhere.
Susan: Do you feel connected to that spirit?
Lindy: Oh, yeah. Definitely! She tunes in every now and then, or I tune into her. It's really nice.
Susan: What happened to your sexual life with Ruth when she was diagnosed?
Lindy: It completely evaporated. Utterly. Neither of us was interested at all. When you hear "cancer," first you're totally shocked, and then you draw in your energy for one purpose, and that's survival. Sex becomes irrelevant. It's like opposite sides of the spectrum: There's love and sex on one side, and there's fear and death on the other. In fact, thinking about it, sex is sort of a luxury that comes with good health. You have to have good physical health and good psychological health in order to have healthy sex.

Through all this, Grace was our number one supporter. So she knew Ruth pretty well, and that's real nice now. She knows what a neat person Ruth was, how wonderful she was.

About a year after Ruth died I started to feel like, well, I don't want to feel like this forever. I need to fill this hole. Relationships are really important for me, and I value them. And I wanted Grace to fill that void.

We had a lot of this [Lindy pushes her hands forward,

palms toward me] and this [pulls her hands back, grasping them into fists] for about a year. We had some rough times because I wanted to be lovers — I thought I did — and Grace didn't. Because of her incest stuff, she just could not be sexual. So here we are, I'm dealing with the loss of my lover, after ten years of being together, the grief. And she's dealing with incest. I mean, you're talking big issues!

And we're trying to get together. I mean, now I look back and think, thank God we took our time. I don't think I was emotionally or psychologically ready for a sexual relationship, but I was ready physically. And Grace was a convenient person to fulfill that. She was my friend, and it was clear we were getting closer and closer. And we had talked, "Okay, yes, I'm attracted to you, you're attracted to me. How are we going to proceed? Okay, you have your incest, I have my grief, this is crazy, yet, still, there's an attraction."

But she said, "No. I have to wait. No matter what that means to you, I have to wait." Which really was a strong statement. And I was just [Lindy makes whiny sounds], "Why don't you give me what I need, and what I want?" Part of me was really respecting her decision, but part of me was, "goddammit!"

We had some big old battles. "How can I be close to you if we're not going to be sexual?" "Well I can't be sexual." This went on for months and months. Finally, we went to therapy together.

Susan: Did you find an answer to, How can I be close to you if we're not being sexual?

Lindy: Yes. The way I found was, first of all, to accept that she couldn't be. It was just so unbelievable to me that incest can even exist. I mean, I never for a minute did not believe her, but on the other hand, I didn't want to believe her, that something this awful could happen! It was so outside my frame of reference, and I hated ... hate, I should say, present tense ... her father. With a fucking passion. And I hate her loyalty, still, to her father.

So, one answer was believing her and accepting that, if I want to be close to her, we have to do something else. So we did massage, which was really nice and erotic, but not threatening. I bought her a massage table, and we both took a massage class. We had real good boundaries, "Okay, this is going to be a nonsexual massage."

Susan: What is the line between a sexual and a nonsexual massage?

Lindy: Well, both people have to agree where that line is. "Does this make you feel uncomfortable, because of the incest, or for any other reason, and if it does, I won't do it." So there's communication. And certain areas are off-limits. You don't rub breasts or in the vagina or pelvic area or bum area. And no kissing. So I learned a lot about communicating sexually with Grace, and I had to learn how to respect her. That was a complete new experience to me, to have to wait. I wanted to just jump on her and do it!

Susan: You could have gone off and found somebody else.

Lindy: Yeah, that's right. I think what kept me in there was our intimacy. We made a little club called the Talk Club. It was just she and I. Now that I think about it, it was so cute! We'd just talk and talk and talk and talk about *every*thing. That was the basis of our relationship. When things got a little rough, and we wouldn't want to talk, we'd say, "Remember the Talk Club." Then we would be able to be open with one another again. I loved that. I needed that desperately, after Ruth died. I needed a good friend, to just spill all this grief, and cry, and talk about feelings. That was our real bond, talking about our feelings. And that's a real way to get intimate with somebody.

Susan: Can you reflect on the difference between becoming intimate with somebody through talk, and becoming intimate with somebody through sex?

Lindy: With talk, with intimacy without the sex, you are developing a closeness that just physical contact can't provide. Then sex is the frosting, and not the main dish. It's a much richer kind of experience. We were really developing a long-term connection with one another. We had so much history, short but intense history. So when we were finally sexual, it was really fantastic. And we know we'll always be the closest of friends.

Susan: How long was this period of becoming intimate without sex?

Lindy: From the time Ruth died until the time we were sexual, I think it was two years.

Susan: How did it happen that you became sexual?

Lindy: We went on a trip to the Southwest in March, and it was beautiful. On the airplane I asked, "Well, do you think this is going to be it? Are we going to be able to be sexual now?" I was always the person to keep it going.

So we got to New Mexico, and set up our tent in some campground. The next day we went on a hike. We got our water and everything and had started up the trail when Grace got something in her eye. I took the water bottle and was leaning over her, pouring water on her eye to help soothe it, and for some reason, right then and there, she said, "I want to make love to you." I said, "Really?" And she said, "Yeah. All the way." "Okay, okay, great," I said. We couldn't do it right there on the trail, so we hiked a little way into the woods. I remember the smell of the pine trees. We laid out a blanket and she took her shirt off. I'm thinking, Oh man, this is great. Because she has nice, large breasts. Oooh, beautiful. So then I took her shorts off, and we just started kissing and loving and licking and everything. It was great! Really nice.

And then this whole family goes trooping by! We had to hide a little bit, because they were only maybe forty feet away. But they were talking and the kids were laughing and they just kind of went on, without seeing us. So that was funny, and the very first time!

When we got back to Minnesota, I was really flipped. I'd been sexual with Grace, and what did that mean about my loyalties to Ruth? And that whole first year Grace's incest stuff would come up sometimes. There were a lot of feelings for quite a while.

Susan: What are some things you have to be especially sensitive about, being the sexual partner of an incest survivor?

Lindy: You have to be flexible and sensitive to what she needs whenever it happens. She used to have actual flashbacks, and then you just need to stop. And sometimes I'm thinking about her incest, and I can say to myself, Oh, just get that out of your mind, but other times I have to say to her, "I think I want to stop; this doesn't feel right."

I have to not be forceful at all. And if I want to suggest new things to try sexually, I have to make sure it's okay. And just talking. As much talking as possible. And also not talking, if she doesn't want to talk about it and I do, which is often the case. And don't talk about incest in bed, or when you've got a meal in front of you. The best place to talk is on a walk, where she's free and not hemmed in, where we can both be on our own two feet.

The thing about being sexual with Grace is — this was new to me — she likes to talk as we're being sexual. She wants to make sure she's present and not dissociated like with the incest. And I don't like to talk so much because I lose my concentration.

Susan: Your concentration on what?

Lindy: Well, right before and during an orgasm, I'm out in the cosmos. I'm connecting with the whole, with the spirit of everything. Sometimes it's visual, I see stars in the sky, and sometimes I'm just out there. I really like leaving. It feels like I'm tuning in to the great force of life. Because it feels to me like an orgasm *is* your life force.

I've told Grace this, and she says in a tiny little voice, "Well, where am I, aren't I there?" And she is, she enables me to get there. The love between us is what's creating that power.

Susan: We've talked a lot about intimacy and not being sexual. What about intimacy and being sexual?

Lindy: When I'm in the mood, and we're being sexual, I feel like I'm really close to Grace. And I like being close. When I'm in the mood, and we're not being sexual, I feel us drifting apart, and I get nervous and scared. Then the minute we're together sexually, I feel closer again. We're really kissy-wissy and huggy-wuggy all the time, and I sometimes think all of that cuddleness is nice, but it's different than being really sexual, being naked and going for it.

Susan: What's different about it?

Lindy: Actually making love is reserved just for Grace. I can be pally-wally and cuddly with a good friend, but the experience of making love is just for Grace. I save it for Grace.

Susan: What's your absolute favorite thing to do sexually?

Lindy: You mean so far?

Susan: Right!

Lindy: One of my favorite things — I'm getting a little bored with it, because it's what I do most of the time — is rubbing on top of each other. Tribadism, I think it's called. I love that, because then you can feel really close along your whole bodies.

Susan: So what are you rubbing on when you're rubbing?

Lindy: On her clit, mostly. We get in a position where our clits can rub on each other.

Susan: Would you be on top, or would she be on top?

Lindy: Both. We rotate. I enjoy being on top, but I love having her on top of me too. Because she's strong and big and nice breasts, oooh. I really like sucking on her breasts too, because she really, *really* gets turned on when I do that.

Susan: How often do you make love?

Lindy: Sometimes we make love two or three times a week, and then nothing for two weeks. It probably averages out to once a week, maybe twice a week. Sometimes we have to say, "Okay, tonight let's try it, and see what happens," whether we want to or not. Usually it ends up being really nice. We just have to set some time aside.

I'm starting to feel like I'm getting a little bored with the same old routine, though. We do try a few different things, and I feel like she's more open to experimentation. I say, " Maybe we should try this or . . ." and she says, "Yeah, sure, great." It's kind of scary, though, to me.

Susan: What do you want to try?

Lindy: I'd have to figure out what else is out there, I guess. Maybe some . . . accoutrements, you know what I mean?

Susan: Like sex toys?

Lindy: Yeah. I've never tried any at all or used anything. I think I can still hear my mother!

Susan: That you should be saving yourself for a person, not a gadget?

Lindy: Exactly! But we've been together four years now, so what the heck? Why not try something new? She has performed anal sex on me, and it's great, it's really fun. But she doesn't like it so much on her.

Susan: Do you have fantasies when you're just sitting

around, or when you're masturbating, or when you're having sex, or . . . ?

Lindy: I think this is one of my motivations for a sex toy. Sometimes I have fantasies that I'm a man. And Grace and I were talking about those things where it's kind of like a penis . . .

Susan: Yeah, a dildo.

Lindy: . . . and where you can put it on your body and your hands are free. So that's been the latest thing.

Susan: And you want to be the "man"?

Lindy: Most of the time it feels like that, yeah. And other times I fantasize Grace being the man. But it's more me, I think. Is that unusual?

Susan: No-o-o! It's totally not unusual. If you walked into a sex toy store and asked them for a dildo, they'd think that was the most boring thing. No. What I think is true is that lots of lesbians are nervous about it. Is "nervous" the right word for how you feel?

Lindy: Embarrassed. Ashamed.

Susan: So what is it about the idea of a dildo . . . ?

Lindy: Well, for one thing, it sort of simulates a man, and I'm a lesbian and not supposed to be interested in the man thing. That's probably primary. And secondly, you're supposed to be wonderfully fine with just your partner; you shouldn't need any accessories.

I think it goes back to being ashamed of being lesbian and not having role models and not having positive examples of our full lives. So we have to be surreptitious about our interests or desires. It's crazy.

I guess it scares me, though, to introduce something new like that. It's just unknown.

Susan: And why would it be scary?

Lindy: I'm sure some of the fear is homophobic in origin, because we lesbians are not supposed to be doing what we're doing, no matter what we're doing. There's some deep-seated stuff there, which pisses me off when I think about it.

The other part is that men scare me sometimes. So it's scary to think that a dildo is simulating a man. And, even though I've never been raped, the idea of rape terrifies me. So I think I would have to be really careful.

Susan: Penises are very powerful images in our culture, and there's a lot of violence associated with them. So then you get one as a toy, and you say, "This is a *toy*?"

Lindy: It's like getting a machine gun as a toy!

Thinking very psychologically about all this, when I'm on top of Grace, and having that fantasy, it's a really strong feeling, that powerful, muscular . . . that "masculine" part of me. And I know she really likes that too, when I'm strong, and have my muscles. So that side comes out with the image, and that's okay.

I think that power has really been used against us as women, so this is a way to get that power back, to use it with us and to use it for us, you know? I mean, choosing whatever it is that we want to use sexually is a real conscious choice of power, or strength, or decisiveness. And fuck 'em if they don't like it.

You know, as I talk about this, it's sounding more and more interesting! I like this idea!

Laura

"That's what we're all about, you know.
Queer people are a little perverse."

Laura: My partner and I thought we were a vibrator store, but we're a dildo store. We sell more silicone dildos than any other product. Next in order of sales are leather harnesses for dildos, then books, then vibrators, either the battery or the plug-in varieties.

Susan: Lots of lesbians are buying dildos?

Laura: Oh yes. They vary from absolutely blushingly nervous to collectors, women who have lots and lots of sex toys, lots of dildos. Mostly people are pretty cool about it, but there's still a lot of education to do when women come in, explaining how harnesses work, and why silicone is better than other kinds of dildos, that it's easy to keep clean and it heats up. That's the part I think is great about silicone. When it's going in and out, in and out, it's just getting hotter and hotter; it feels really good.

It's a lot more expensive, though. I think it's really the cleanliness that sells it; it's a respectful material. Silicone dildos are prettier too, and made mostly by women. They're high-quality fucker ware. And there's a new generation of people who really want them.

Laura is a thirty-one-year-old woman, tall and slim, with short, sandy-blonde hair. She is the co-owner of The Rose-Wet Cave, an upscale sex-toy store in a gay-friendly neighborhood of Atlanta. Laura is thus professionally — as well as personally — familiar with dildos of every shape, size, style, and color.

Laura and I are talking in the backroom of her store, which has the businesslike feel of any other office space. But out front, where the merchandise is displayed, the mood changes. Jazz is playing quietly. The large room is well lit with track lighting and two large windows that front on the street, but the decor gives an enclosed, protected, warm, and sensuous feeling to the room. The ceiling is painted black, the walls different shades of red, rose, and pink. The carpet is rose red, the display shelves and cabinets black. And every shelf and cabinet is filled to overflowing with a wide variety of sex toys, as well as sex-oriented books, magazines, videos and cards, scents and oils, safe-sex supplies and lubricants.

I count ninety dildos, some shaped like penises (with and without testicles), some shaped like fingers or corncobs, in red, pink, purple, black, and Caucasian and

African-American flesh colors. There are twenty-two styles of dildo harnesses in red, blue, black, and purple; forty-seven kinds of vibrators; forty-five styles of butt plugs. There are paddles and whips, chains and handcuffs, nipple clips and cock rings.

Laura and her co-owner and their employees move serenely through this mass of evocative material, talking matter-of-factly with customers, suggesting the perfect item to meet their needs.

Susan: Tell me something about the different kinds of dildo harnesses.

Laura: There are different styles, like a G-string style that is an up-the-crack thong sort of thing. There are harnesses with two straps, one around each thigh. They come in different materials, nylon and leather and denim. The customer ... you, for instance, have to pick what you like, what says sex to you. I have to introduce that thought to people who don't go into sex stores a lot, introduce them to feeling okay about what they like, and really choosing from their gut.

People are pretty cool about it, though we do get customers who are completely blown away. There was this one woman who was standing in the restraints area, whips and paddles and chains, where most people don't even go because it pushes some button. She's standing in the S/M area sort of twiddling her thumbs. I come up to her and say, "Can I help you find anything?" She says, "No-o-o. Uhhh. Over there," and points to the dildos. Now it's not like she's fine with S/M stuff, it's just that that stuff doesn't remotely signify sex to her, like the dildos do, which is her ultimate desire. So she's hiding in the S/M section, twenty feet away from the dildos.

To make conversation with her I say, "What do you do?" And she says, "I'm a sex educator." Here she is, teaching about fallopian tubes and spermatozoa, and her desire is foreign to her, terrifying to her. It's so sad; we're just not okay with desire.

Susan: How did you decide to do your store?

Laura: I was introduced to sex toys by a girlfriend, and I enjoyed them and liked having lubricants. But I couldn't find the lube I liked best in any local store. At the same time my closest friend, Ginny, was just graduating from business school and was scheming about how to make a living, how to make it all pay off. When she heard me complaining about not being able to find the lube, she was just on it like that [Laura snaps her fingers].

I knew it was a really good business idea, I saw the vision as clear as day, brilliant sunlight on this vision. But it was very hard to keep the vision clear because there wasn't a sex store here, and none of my friends except Ginny really understood what I was up to. It was kind of scary. And it disrupted my family. My father was really awful about it, but my brothers supported me 100 percent. One of them even named the store, from one of Adrienne Rich's *Twenty-One Love Poems*.

Susan: And what is your vision?

Laura: That every city needs a store that is friendly and informative and carries high-quality sex toys and is integrated into the city. There's this whole tolerant portion of the population — women and men, straight and gay and lesbian and bisexual — who just want to have a place to go for sex toys that doesn't make them feel like they have to take a shower after they go there.

We try to give off this feeling that you can ask us anything. People have nothing but questions about sex. Everybody wants the opportunity to talk about it.

Susan: What are some of the most frequent questions people ask?

Laura: Will I stop being able to come with a partner if I use a vibrator? Will I go numb? Will I have all the orgasms I possibly can with the vibrator and never have another one with a person? I tell them that the beauty of the clitoris is that it's organic, it regenerates; orgasms are like a renewable resource. So you won't wear out your clitoris. Just don't use the vibrator as much when you're about to have a date with somebody. Or bring it into your sex play if you want to.

People want to know, What are butt plugs for? Why would anybody want to do that? For women it's that the clitoris is just the tip of the iceberg. It has these legs or roots, this whole elaborate system of erectile tissue, that goes all the way around the vagina and then around the anus. So in sex all this blood gets flowing, and the whole system becomes engorged. Then when you introduce something into the anus, everything else tightens up and gets hotter. It's like a clitoral response in the anus.

Then there's the general pleasure in pooping. There are endorphins released when you're pooping that feel good, so when you're putting something in and out and in and out of the anus, you're getting those endorphins over and over again.

People are wired differently, though, and some people just don't like anal sex at all. And other people will never get over the mental baggage, which is maybe fine too if they're having other fun sex. So, anal sex is a mysterious great unknown taboo sex-play area that people like to talk about, or like to avoid talking about.

Susan: What else is available that people like once they know about it?

Laura: The restraints and sensation toys, like light and heavy floggers, paddles, canes, tit clamps, blindfolds, all the S/M accoutrements.

The S/M community spends more money on sex than anybody else. They are just sold on it. They just want it all. Once people figure out that they want to play around with that stuff, it's a big identity thing, another widely misunderstood, hated, and feared identity. Once people cross into it, it's just like being gay, another kind of coming out.

Laura talks easily and knowledgeably about her merchandise and customers, anonymously of course, and with nearly equal ease when we talk about the details of her own sex life. She recounts her sexual experiences graphically and dramatically, dropping her head on her arms, burying her face in her hands, throwing her arms wide. She is somewhat more halting when we discuss her love life, a domain where she feels less expertise. Her voice becomes more quiet, her forehead wrinkles in concentration, her gestures contract.

Susan: What do you remember about sex from your childhood? What were your family's attitudes about sex?

Laura: Well, my family was all men — my mom died when I was two years old — so my father raised me and my two older brothers. Sex was really never talked about at all, although I think my father was kind of liberal about it. One day when I was eleven or twelve, he and I were driving along in Colorado, where I'm from, listening to the radio, and a song came on about sex, about kissing all over or something, and I went "Ee-o-oh, yuck," like a kid. He said, "You know, it's a really nice thing to do." He was talking about the sensuality of it. I was really shocked, and remember that to this day.

He actually got married again to get me through puberty because he was kind of scared of women. When I was going to get my period, he didn't know what to do. So he just sort of picked up a wife, though she and I didn't talk about sex at all.

I learned about sex from books. I learned how to masturbate from a book. I'm so happy about that! So pleased! I remember one day when I was ten or eleven, it was this beautiful day, we had bought roller skates for me. I remember going to bed and starting to masturbate, and it just going on forever and ever and ever, never really having an orgasm, but that wasn't the point; it felt like flying, I was just *so* happy and turned on and young.

There was an exotic aspect to being a girl in my family. There was all this masculine power being thrown around, and I had to fit in between the cracks, be smart and athletic and stuff like that. I felt vulnerable, like I had to get through it, had to feel safe if I could. No one ever did anything bad to me exactly, but I was sexualized, like girls are. My father wanted me to grow up normal and girl-like, he was just treating a girl like a girl. But like all the men of his generation, girls are sexual, that's our main difference from men. So sex is right there, all the time. I feel this sort of kinship with people who are survivors of incest, even though I know I'm not one. But in a general cultural sense, it's absolutely there for me. I learned how to get along sexually and to get around sexually.

Susan: When you were growing up, did you like boys? Did you like girls?

Laura: Oh, I liked me [she laughs]. That's the truth, because I feel like my sexuality is just outlaw. I wanted men, and I wanted girls and women, but never boys. Boys were so obnoxious and immature. But I did get crushes on teachers, exclusively male teachers. I had a big crush on a teacher when I was in junior high school. Then when I was high-school age I went away to boarding school and developed this giant crush on another teacher. This one came to fruition.

Sexually it was just so forbidden. He was married. He was a teacher, I was a student. He was twenty-seven, I was sixteen. Of course I was much older than my years, and he was a child. But he was really great sexually, though I don't think I ever had an orgasm with him. He tried, he went down on me and stuff like that, but he didn't romance me enough for me to understand what was going on. I remember thinking, What's he doing? Oh my god. This feels really weird! But it was thrilling. Totally exciting.

Susan: Exciting sexually or exciting emotionally?

Laura: Exciting in an adventure kind of way. And sexually too. I don't know why that cunnilingus moment didn't work out. When I think about it, it was the perfect relationship for me, forbidden, and nowhere private to be sexual, and all this excitement, and power being exchanged. It was great. Everything I loved then, I pretend is true when I have sex now.

Susan: When did you first become attracted to women or girls?

Laura: Well, when I was sixteen, I had this nagging doubt about this affliction called lesbianism. A girl on my high-school softball team came out in front of everyone — she also was named Laurie — and I thought, with my luck that's me too.

I didn't want to be a lesbian. I was pretty, but I was a depressed, negative kind of child in a lot of ways. I had a lot of problems. And I wasn't normal, I didn't feel normal. I wasn't dating boys, I was having my totally adult subversive sex life on the side, concealed from everyone.

But years went by before anything happened about being a lesbian. Once I got to college I went to the Women's Center, a well-established radical place, and my entire life changed. That was my epiphany, becoming a feminist. A lot of lesbians say, "Oh, I kissed a girl and bombs burst in air," but for me it was totally painful and awful to kiss a girl. But to become a feminist... the scales fell from my eyes. I remember thinking, Now I can understand everything that was so baffling before. So I'm a political lesbian, I think.

Susan: How was becoming a feminist relevant to becoming a lesbian?

Laura: Feminism provided this atmosphere, this woman culture. It was like a kindergarten for my sexuality, because it was safe to talk about lesbianism. It was safe to become close to women. I became inseparable from Ashley, my first girlfriend. She taught me how to talk about myself. She was a sort of mom/therapist, the I-can-save-you-from-yourself kind of thing.

Susan: How did you wind up being sexual with her?

Laura: It's funny you should ask that because some friends and I were just discussing how hard it can be for lesbians to decide when the first time was they "had sex" with a woman. "Being sexual" I think we all know, but "having sex" . . . the main event for lesbians is so different, there's just such a variety. It's so great that way, not so singular and phallic. We decided "having sex" for lesbians was "digits in the fertile delta," you know, hands in cunts.

Anyway, my friend Ashley and I were fighting because she thought I was a homophobe. We slept together in the same bed and denied all of our sexual — or whatever it was that was going on — tension, or intention. At the same time I had lots of boyfriends, who all turned out to be gay. It was so confusing. I would not put my worst enemy through adolescence.

You could cut the tension between Ashley and me with a knife. We were like tigers in a cage, or scorpions in a jar, like, Who's going to kill who? Then one day I just crawled in bed with her and made a pass. I squished her up against the wall and kissed her. I must have felt some desire, but it was also in response to this really awful emotional situation. Later she blamed me for our lesbianism.

Susan: So it wasn't a fun, wonderful kind of thing?

Laura: No. My first orgasm, though, Oh my god! My first orgasm that somebody else gave me, I mean. The scene was totally unromantic, totally utilitarian, I think Ashley even said something like, "Here goes nothing," and then it was incredible. The orgasm was just incredible. It made me want to have sex for the rest of my life. I felt it like this electric current in my fingertips, this buzzing in my toes. It was just overwhelmingly pleasurable.

So I became a happily sexual person, although I went through about two weeks of breaking out from stress about it. I just couldn't stand to think that I was a lesbian. My identity never really did gel.

Susan: Why did you decide that you were a lesbian?

Laura: Because it was so in the air. Everyone was talking about it. There were lesbians in my life, and I thought, Am I one of Them? I felt instead like, I sleep with girls but I'm not a lesbian.

I still have that idea. I think it's a homophobic little kernel in me, that I think, yeah, there are lesbians, and then there's me. Like on one level — the who-I'm-going-to-have-sex-with level — I'm 100 percent identified with being lesbian. But on the cultural level, it's just not enough for me and never was enough. There are people for whom identifying as a lesbian is the key, the thing that everything else in their lives rests on. But I felt identified against most of the lesbians I knew. It must have been aesthetic . . . I don't know . . . I . . . I think it's homophobia, that's the reason. Being a lesbian is a bad thing to be.

So it's just not something that I wear on my sleeve, but boy do I love the girls that do [she laughs], you know, like the ones who are born that way. I'm into them! That's the sexiest thing in the world is to be a lesbian, like a dyke, whose whole sexuality is right there.

Susan: Do you mean butch? Or do you mean born lesbian?

Laura: Born lesbian. Though butch also helps. There's something so sexy about born lesbians. And just to have it resolved. I don't think that I'm going to change, because I don't have that core experience. I have all this man stuff in my past or in my psyche or something.

Susan: What do you mean "man stuff?"

Laura: Desire for men, relations with men. Like my whole growing up was in relation to men. They're this whole other part of the world that I can't forget about. But I prefer women so much. I've set up my entire life where I don't have to be around men. When I am, it's bizarre, strange, just another world altogether. But that's my homeland. I like to say that I was raised by wolves. And I'm just learning the ways of people now.

Susan: Tell me about a time you made love with a woman that you really liked.

Laura: It was last night, about nine hours ago. What do you want to know?

Susan: All the details. Where you were, and who seduced whom, and . . .

Laura: Well, for about a month I've been dating one of those born lesbians. I am more into her, like sexually, than I can remember *ever* being into anybody.

Susan: What does she look like?

Laura: She is a stud, a fox, totally beautiful. Oh my god, it's awful. I can't stand to be around her. She's so foxy. Ask anybody. She's a couple of years younger than me, and taller by a little bit. She's got a beautiful, beautiful face, blue eyes, brown hair, and she's big, her body is big, heavy, solid. She's the sexiest thing on legs. She channels some power. Seriously.

Last night we went to a play with friends, and things just got out of hand. Usually we decide ahead of time when we're going to see each other and whether we're going to hang out — like go to a movie — or if we're going on a date, which means we're going to have sex. That way both of us know what's going on. We haven't really been hanging out much because we just have sex all the time because it's so sexy.

Anyway, we have a date today, after I finish talking to you. We're going to spend the whole day fucking around, you know, until we get too hungry. But last night, after the show, she said, "I need to go use the bathroom in your store," which of course means we're going to have sex at the store. We came here — she's always wanted to do that, because I own the store and it's a sex store and it's sexy — and went into the back room over there [she points to a door that is ajar] where people try on dildo harnesses. She starts sexing me up, kissing me and stuff. Then she took my pants off and said, "I want to make you come like crazy in your own store." So then she started licking on me, that's my favorite thing, the way I come. And it helps to have something in my asshole too, so she puts her finger in there and moves it around a little bit, not too much. So that's the way it went.

Susan: Did you make love to her too?

Laura: Oh yes. We have this exceptional relationship where she's sort of a top, and I'm sort of a bottom, but only sort of. She's not like stone or anything, she likes to get pleasured. So she agreed to me going down on her too, and I did. Then she did me again. We were there for a long time. On the floor. It was so sexy. It was just so sexy.

Susan: What do you think makes it so sexy?

Laura: The urgency. It's like not being in a relationship. We're keeping the mundane things at bay. Someday I'd like to go through the mundane things with somebody too. I've never done that struggle. It's like there's an expiration date stamped on every single relationship that I have. It just passes — after about a year and a half — and that's it.

There's no negotiating with desire, you know. It's so much better to have those big feelings than not to, but you can't always arrange for that to be true, you can't always be in love, you can't always have a crotch-on-fire kind of desire for your girlfriend. Sometimes it just goes away.

Susan: Do you know why it goes away for you?

Laura: Yes, I'm pretty sure it's an intimacy pattern. I fall in love, the sex gets better, intimacy gets heightened, and then new levels of intimacy come along that I have to reach, and I can't get there. So I stop wanting to have sex, period.

The past couple of days I've been telling all my friends that I think I'm falling in love with this date woman. But I'm not going to tell her because I don't want to ruin what we have made so far.

Susan: Do you mean ruin the sex? Or what do you mean by what you've made?

Laura: I don't know ... [she pauses to think] ... I don't think it would ruin the sex, but she might just leave. That would ruin the sex all right!

Susan: What does it mean when you say you think you're falling in love?

Laura: Well, on the one hand we're friends, and on the other we're lovers, but we're not girlfriends, which is somewhere in the middle. I think it's all kind of starting to flow together, like she's becoming integrated into my life that way. I'm starting to want to talk to her about everything. And it's just deepening, it's just opening up into this whole new thing ... it's taking a turn for the deeper, feeling-wise.

Susan: Does that mean it's becoming more intimate?

Laura: Yeah, I think it is becoming more intimate. [Laura is wrinkling up her nose.]

Susan: Is this a good development or not?

Laura: It's a good thing ... [she sighs] ... I mean, it is. But it's something I have a lot of trouble with. It's something that I was trying not to do this time, that kind of intimacy. Here's the thing: I don't want to do the same thing over again that I have been doing. I want to love her almost independent of who she is. I want the love I have to flow in her direction continuously.

But when I give a name like "girlfriend" to a lover, I start to think, I'm not going to love you if you sleep with someone else. All these little obstacles to love crop up, and I just can't have that. I don't want it.

In the past, whatever I've called it, a relationship or a partnership or girlfriendship, all I want is for them not to want to sleep with anybody else. But they're going to want what they want — you can't control their wanting — and that's going to hurt no matter what label you slap on the relationship. There's nothing I can do about my date's desire. I'm just lucky right now she doesn't want to sleep with anyone else.

Susan: So there's something about falling in love that implies exclusivity?

Laura: To me, it does. I'd like to be hip and modern and not have that be true, but it's true. I see examples of good monogamy and good nonmonogamy, but you have to find your own path and mine is probably going to be monogamous. For me sex is too meaningful, it's too intimate.

I think I might have been okay with my date woman sleeping with other people earlier, before I started to fall in love. At least that's what I had to say to get her to sleep with me. No, I'm kidding. I think I really thought that, but I didn't feel it. Once I got down to what I was feeling, what I feel is, I want her to really want me, not to want anyone else. I want her to really love me, and I want her to love only me.

Susan: Tell me about another favorite sexual time you've had with this woman.

Laura: I'm trying to think. I've fingered them so much in my mind that I can't really pick one out. They're so fun to think about, you know, but then I stop thinking about one because I have another one.

Okay, there was this one recent time — this is going to

blow your doors off — that was so incredibly smooth, including dildos and everything. Just let me say, though, that generally dildos add a dorky aspect to things, like when you have to put them on and take them off. And there's this feminist problem with dildos and penetration that a lot of lesbians have.

Susan: What is the problem?

Laura: That we're mimicking men and we've turned away from men, so why should we put on a dick. What I think is, if you don't want penetration or a dildo, then that's fine. But if you do, you have to get it because it's important to get what you want sexually as a lesbian. It's so important. So I want it, and I know a lot of women who do, that's why we do such a brisk business with dildos and harnesses.

A dildo is also mentally sexy. It's kind of a mind-fuck experience to be thrusting your pelvis, your dildo, into your girlfriend or lover or whomever. It's a little bit perverse, and that's what we're all about, you know. Queer people are a little perverse. We do stuff people don't think is okay.

So, understand, you can feel really dorky putting a dildo on, because sex has this trapping of being natural and naked and flesh on flesh and so on. And here you are putting on equipment. It can often be a comical experience, and you just have to get used to it. You can bring anything into your sex life, anything can be eroticized, much weirder things than dildos. It's a little bit of work to eroticize some things, but if you want it, that's how you have to do it.

So all that being said, then I had this great dildo experience in which there wasn't a dorky moment; it was like out of a movie or something. I came over to my girlfriend's house for pretty much our first date. We were just getting together to have sex, really, still in the golden period where we're not emotionally involved. It was our first arranged date, "Let's get together and have sex all day."

I arrived wearing these red velvet pants and fake zebra belt and this tight little shirt, no natural fibers, all very sleazy. She's sitting over there on the couch just completely exuding sex — I didn't know why at the time, but you'll find out — wearing jeans and some hot shirt. She likes to wear these things that are completely worn out, holes in them and falling off of her. She is delicious! Exotic. Soft.

I was nervous, which is the cool thing about it. She's in charge and I'm the one who's nervous. Thank god! Finally! Here I am, running my whole entire life — running my store, having employees, making sure everything gets paid, dealing with the government — I just want to go get seduced.

So she says, "I'm totally turned on. I'm so turned on," walks over to me and says, "The first thing I want you to do is suck my dick." It turns out she'd had this dildo on all day, walking around at the Safeway, you know, she was just having this totally sexual experience all day.

I'm terrified, I'm so excited. So she whipped it out, and I sucked it. I was astonished at how much I wanted to do that and how far in my mouth, down my throat it went. I thought I was pretty macho, pretty powerful to take in that whole thing. The experience turned out to be so mentally exciting because she's not supposed to want that, and I'm not supposed to want that, both of us being lesbians. It was just an excellent place to start off our first planned date.

And she was very seductive with the dildo. She didn't break the mood. I tend to break the mood, to get kind of goofy, like I ask people, "Do you think this dildo is too long?"

Susan: Have you got several dildos to choose from?

Laura: I have more than several. I mean, I own all those dildos out front in the store, and I can have any one of them. But I have a few favorites.

So then she said, "Go up to my room and take off all your clothes and wait for me on the bed." She had me kneel on all fours on the bed and wait for her, naked, wondering what was going to happen. Then she came up and sat across from me and said things like, "I wonder who knows you're here, showing me your ass like that." Then she just used me, used my body! She fucked me in the vagina with the dildo. Later I got to wear a different dildo and fuck her. The look on her face was just beatific, just sublimely pleasured. It was really like the dildos were integrated into the whole thing, a lot like having a penis around, but one that really behaves, that is not so single-minded, so self-centered, that stays hard and does all the stuff that penises are known not to do.

Then also she had her finger in my ass or maybe it was a butt plug. And she went down on me. And I went down on her. It was like this experience of being so alive in the moment. We were expressing ourselves, not through words but through our physical bodies.

Then later that day, after that whole experience, we started talking about bondage and how I wanted to do that too. I've been tied up. I like being completely ineffectual. I've got a very strong body, and I like for it to be completely incapacitated. I like being forced to have an orgasm, pretend, you know. It's like there's this circuit of power. The more in touch you are with what you want, and the more you get what you want, the more power there is.

Susan: And what do you think the source of that power is?

Laura: I think it's God! It's the life force. Following

your feelings and your desires is part of being a person. It's like agreeing to be fully alive, getting out of the way of life as it wants to exist.

You can get in your own way, you know. You can arrange your life to where you control everything, and it's deadening and boring. Or you can follow your desires, and who knows where they will lead? It's like tapping into something a lot bigger than you, a benevolent power that wants the best for everyone, that wants everyone to be just as satisfied and fully alive as they can be.

Melanie

"I'm a sensation slut. I like lots
of sensations, all at once,
all over the place."

When I was eighteen or nineteen I went to this
goddess gathering in upstate New York — they had a
rebirthing ceremony for the solstice or whatever it was —
and I met this woman. She was like twenty-four, older
than me, and a teacher. She was very fascinating to me. I
spent the night at her house and we cuddled, but we
didn't kiss. This was one of those lesbian one-nighters
where, you know, you spend the night and don't do
anything. But the touching we did do was that kind when

you touch someone's face and their mouth and their ears and their fingertips and it's all electric. It goes right to your pussy, and there's no stopping it. Somehow I think that's the key to sex, that electricity, that passion, that tension, that anxiety. It was all touch and nervousness and feelings of "I want to but I just can't." I felt the way I had earlier in my life, when I wanted someone to just jump on me.

Melanie is an attractive twenty-five-year-old woman, small and slim, with shoulder-length black hair and dark eyes. She is wearing a touch of coral lipstick and mint-green eye shadow. She moves with grace, assurance, and perfect posture, a reflection of her years of training as a dancer. Melanie currently works part-time as a stripper, supplementing the work she does in an AIDS organization. She was raised in New York City, the daughter of an educated and liberal Jewish family. Melanie now considers her moderately spiritual orientation to be, as she described it, "Eclectic, Judeo, Twelve-Step, Star Trek, Gaia, etc."

I met Melanie in the large house she shares with her lover, Joan, another woman, a gay man, a German shepherd, and several cats in a multicultural neighborhood near the University of Pennsylvania in downtown Philadelphia. She is a calm, self-possessed, and loquacious young woman, accustomed to talking about sex, eager to describe the variety of her experience in graphic detail; she loves the dramatic. She lets me know at the end of the interview, "I'm trying to be the sex radical to add to your spectrum."

Susan: What was your family's attitude toward sex?
Melanie: My parents were hippies, so they were very open and direct. I always knew what a vagina was. I felt

like I understood what was going on with sex and with my body pretty clearly.

Susan: Were you attracted to boys? To girls?

Melanie: I was very attracted to boys, the standard heterosexual girl kind of thing. I had crushes and obsessed about, Am I skinny enough? and, Is my hair right? Though looking back I can identify all the crushes I had on girls. I was completely obsessed with one girl from first to third grade. She was so pretty, white-blonde hair, really different from me. In third grade she dogged me — you know, dropped me — for another best friend, and from that moment on I absolutely despised her and was fascinated with her. This obsession has continued. I know where she went to college and what she's doing now.

When I was about fifteen I started feeling like boys were gross in a really profound way. I had read *Rubyfruit Jungle*, and it changed my whole world. After I read that I just kept thinking, Men are frogs, men are frogs, meaning their genitalia are gross. My lesbian persona, my emotional identification with women, was beginning to be very strong at that age.

There was a dance teacher I was in love with when I was in junior high school. She was Central American, dark, dark black and so beautiful. Slim shoulders, incredibly powerful legs, muscular but just flowing. I thought she was the most amazing thing I'd ever seen in my life, and she was a lesbian. I worshiped her.

All my friends were kissing boys at this point, but I would not kiss them. It was so gross to me, tongues touching, saliva, like spitting in somebody else's mouth. And I was obsessed with doing it right, like I didn't want to kiss if I wasn't going to be a good kisser.

I really just wanted someone else to take control, I wanted someone to make me kiss them so I could get over that hump. But I kept dating boys who were much too nice. Then the summer after tenth grade, I was fifteen, I found myself a boyfriend and kissed him a lot. He was really gross, and I couldn't stand him, but I kissed him a lot anyway. At the end of that summer I decided I was going to have sex, so I found a boy that I liked and did it. I don't remember very much, but I do remember thinking that his penis was really pokey and like a pencil. And it was not that exciting. I remember thinking, "I'm just too young for this. How am I going to get any enjoyment out of this? I'm just not ready." But I'd flirt with boys because I didn't know how to be friends without flirting. So I'd get myself into pickles . . . a lot.

The next couple of years I went out with boys and either slept with them or didn't, but my big thing was conquest; I tried to sleep with all these virgins. It started to get kind of entertaining, but you know, boys have a really Coke bottle agenda about sex; they just want to squeeze their dick into a Coke bottle. I had a lot of erotic energy, like, Yes, I do want to fuck, but also, How come I'm never getting off?

Susan: Did you worry about safe sex?

Melanie: I didn't worry about AIDS yet, I was worried about other sexually transmitted diseases and getting pregnant. My mom knew I was having sex; she would let me have boys over to spend the night. She said, "If you're going to be having sex, then I think we should talk about the kind of birth control you will need." She took me to get a diaphragm and bought me condoms. The condom was a really good way for me to avoid the whole fluid issue, because I was never that excited about semen. I think I might have given head three times in my life; that whole concept totally grossed me out.

I finally had a really erotic experience with a boy when I was eighteen. I had had a huge crush on him in high school — he was on the football team, and I was a cheerleader — but he had another girlfriend. So he and I got to be kind of flirty pals. Later he went away to college and, even though I was still in high school, I called him up and went to visit him. He still had the same girlfriend, whom I knew.

When I got to his dorm, he came out to meet me and picked me up into the air and spun me around in circles and kissed me. He introduced me to his roommates, who then made themselves scarce, and we kissed for like ever, and must have made out for hours and hours. Somewhere in the middle of the night we decided we were going to have sex, and he said the classiest line any boy has ever said to me, he said, "Shall we dress for the occasion?" I thought that was so suave.

So I was, like, "Okay, let's go!" It was the first really good sex I had with a boy. I loved it and had so much fun. I think part of the reason I had such a good time is that he went down on me. It was all just so sordid and bad, and the badness of it was really good!

Looking back on it all it's so funny to me. Because I was such a drama queen. I think I was a drama queen until about two years ago. [Pause. Melanie tilts her head, raises her chin and looks directly at me.] I might still be one now.

Susan: Where is your attraction for girls in all this?

Melanie: Well, back when I was fifteen my best friend in the entire universe was this girl Sally. It was like I had found my soul mate. She understood everything about me, and I understood everything about her; when we ate together we always gave each other the best bite and the last bite. And we were compassionate toward each other, because she had this horrible naggy mom, and my dad was a drunk. We were on the phone constantly. We wrote notes, we wrote in each other's diaries, we read each other's diaries. It was very classic. And we talked a lot about bisexuality. We had friends our age, girls, who were sleeping with each other. We were fascinated by that, and wanted to be better friends with them.

Susan: Was bisexuality a positive thing?

Melanie: We were nervous about it, but it was cool. At this time we were going to a public school that was an arts school — I had gotten in by auditioning for the dance program — and there were faggy boys and obvious lesbians who were out about it. Sally and I spent a lot of time talking about girls at school, "Is she a dyke?" "She's got to be a dyke."

Susan: Did you consider yourself heterosexual, or did you not think about categories at all?

Melanie: Well, I knew I was bisexual.

Susan: How did you know that?

Melanie: Because I knew I liked girls.

Susan: So even though you weren't doing anything with them . . .

Melanie: Oh, I knew I didn't have to *do* something.

Then I went away to college, to the University of Illinois, and was really radical. I was this hippie. I was weird looking, my tie-dyes, my beads, all this crystal munchkin stuff. I had really radical politics, and I talked a lot about sex.

Sally came out to visit me when I was there. She stayed a couple of days, and when she left she kissed me, full in the mouth. And I'm like, "No, I don't want this. This isn't what I want our relationship to be." It didn't feel right to me; it felt like kissing my best friend. It was gucky.

Also at Illinois I was stunned by the fact that about 30 to 50 percent of the women I met my first year had been raped at some point in their lives, date rape or stranger rape or incest. It was just bizarre. I began feeling a sense of compassion and a real sense of wrong about men and

penises, and I started thinking more about bisexuality. My
boyfriend back home thought it was really cute.

Susan: He thought what was really cute?

Melanie: Bisexuality. He thought it was really cute that
I kind of liked girls. He was condescending and trite, and
when I came home for Christmas I had gained a couple of
pounds, and he was furious. I broke up with him a couple
of months later. And then I had a little almost-fling with
my first girl.

It was at this point, back home in New York City, that
Melanie went to the goddess gathering where she and a
woman teacher spent the night together, Melanie's
"almost-fling." Rather than return to the University of
Illinois — "Everyone in downstate Illinois is so fucking
repressed," she explained — she transferred to the
University of Pennsylvania.

Melanie: I knew I was going to Penn to be queer. That
was part of my agenda. I'm going to leave my world
behind, and I'm going to be queer here.

Susan: How did you know?

Melanie: I don't know. I just knew.

I had dreadlocks, and I didn't shave my legs or my
armpits and didn't wear makeup. I developed this crush on
a senior rower girl — I was being a coxswain for the crew
team — who was kinda big and burly and butch looking, a
very interesting face, not at all a feminine-looking face. I
liked her a lot and hung out with her. And eventually I
came out to her. Then she started dating a girl, and I was
totally miserable.

I fooled around with this one guy, who is not very
interesting, except that was the first time I ever did "pearl
necklace," where the boy jacks off between your breasts,
comes all over your throat. That was an experience.

That next summer back home in New York I met this woman who said she had told everybody she was straight, but she was interested in me. We hung out a lot, and became girlfriends at the end of the summer. We kissed a lot. She was the hipbone kind of girl, she liked to grind on people's hipbones. That's just not my way of sex; the rubbing doesn't get me anywhere. I'm much more of a penetration queen.

We had this passionate affair, and it was totally secret. At the same time I was hooked up with this boy that had had a crush on me in high school. Bob was saying, "I don't want to be with you if you're with somebody else," and Gail was saying, "I'll take whatever you can give me." I felt Bob had a much healthier attitude, so I broke up with her and dated him.

That same summer my mom had been reading about Queer Nation — this direct action queer political movement — in the newspaper and been telling me about it, that there was this funny group, with these great actions. They've got boys dressed up in nun outfits, and so on. She thought they were the coolest thing and was totally psyched out for me to be in Queer Nation. So, when I went back to college for my junior year I became involved with Queer Nation, which totally changed my universe. And through them I found out about the queer safety patrol, which was a bunch of dykes and fags who put on uniforms and little berets and marched around the streets, intervening to prevent hate crimes against queers.

The chapter coordinator in Philadelphia, Tracey, was this foxy young activist dyke — she was about eighteen, and I was about twenty — that I became obsessed with. She was all butch and fierce and had this little swagger. It was really exciting to me. I found out that she went to Queer Nation meetings, so what really lured me there more than anything else was my pussy. She gave her little report, and she's wearing this nice button-down-the-front shirt and cute glasses. I was just lost. I did everything I possibly could to flirt with her, I was relentless.

Susan: What would you do to flirt with her?

Melanie: Look at her longer than usual, and bat my eyes at her, and stare at her, and be really coy, and place myself strategically, and suck in my stomach and purse my lips . . . I'm being a little facetious now. [We laugh.] I used all my flirting skills that I had learned all those years of luring boys in. And it worked, because she called me, and we made a date.

Now this had an interesting twist to it. I had just moved into a new group-living situation, where most of the people were couples, except me and Jeffrey, who were singles. One night we stayed up really late talking and ended up having sex. I woke up the next morning and thought, Oh god. And then Tracey calls to make a date for the next day.

I kept having this sense of my body being contaminated by this boy and not wanting to be near her until I felt like my body was clean. I kept thinking it takes twenty-seven days for your cells to completely replace themselves. I just knew I wasn't going to have that much time, but I was really stressing about this cell issue.

So we met for our date in a park and started doing the lesbian flirt things, playing with each other's hair and giving each other back rubs. She had this long hair at the time which I thought was so fierce, so sexy. We were swinging on the swings and talking and talking. Then it was getting dark, and we're standing by the car, and she says, "Come home with me now." She had kissed me already. And she whispered all these amazing things in my ear, like, "You're never going to forget my name," and "I'll give you the best you ever had." These total assertions of self-confidence. I thought they were the sexiest thing I'd ever heard and was just enraptured.

And I refused to go home with her, I said I'd call her

tomorrow. She couldn't believe it, she was stunned. I guess no one had ever said no. So I went over the next day.

Susan: Why did you say no that night?

Melanie: Well, partly because I wanted to make her wait. And because I wanted to make myself wait. And because I was nervous; I felt like I hadn't really had sex with a girl yet, so I didn't know what I was going to do. And it was the clean thing, I didn't feel like my body was ready. But it was also this control issue, I felt like I had to control the situation because she was overwhelming. Just really attractive; I was fucked up for her.

Susan: When you say she was really butch, what does that mean?

Melanie: I consider myself a femme, not quite a high femme, but I can be. And I have this thing for butch girls. I have tried to dress butch and be butch. I spent a couple of weeks focusing on being butch, I cut my hair off, wore button-down-the-front shirts, made my tits really flat, wore blocky shoes, changed my whole walk. I did a lot to try and be butch and it was really unsuccessful, really ineffective. I looked like a really pretty short-haired girl. I just didn't fit my image of what butch was.

For me butch is partly about being masculine, having a boyish demeanor and a boyish look and a boyish walk, and part of it is about feeling almost uncomfortable in a girl's body. Like girly things are totally repulsive to this type of woman. You would never see her wearing a dress and heels, and if you did, she would look terribly out of place and really uncomfortable. She would tend to wear grandma underwear, big old high-waisted underwear or boxers. And I like big girls, girls that are strong in their shoulders and have thick legs, really substantial thighs. Skinny girls don't get me anywhere.

Something about the way a butch girl sits with her legs apart is sexy. And the way they walk in this determined, don't-fuck-with-me way. It's totally not delicate. Delicate flower would be the reverse.

Susan: How would you describe your being a femme?

Melanie: Well, I want the butch who's with me to put her arm around me protectively, and to feel proud that she's taking care of me because I am so fierce. I want to be treated like I'm the most delicate flower with the sharpest nails.

I don't any more think that being a femme has to do with my hair length or whether or not I wear lipstick. I think it has more to do with how I feel about my body and how I feel about the kinds of clothes I wear or the way I walk, the way I wiggle. I think being femme is partly about being feminine in a kind of traditional girly way, accessing and manipulating that kind of stereotypical femininity to one's own advantage. Knowing that I can put on lipstick and makeup and heels and a pushup bra and just knock people dead, that's really satisfying, the sex appeal kind of gig.

When I move my body, like in sex, I'm conscious of female movements, very sensual and slow and girly. And whether I'm on my back or my side or on my hands and knees, I'm conscious of wanting to look like a porn star. It makes me feel sexier to act sexier, that blur between the image and the reality comes in. Part of that comes from having been a dancer and a stripper and seeing my body in mirrors, knowing what I look like in all kinds of good positions doing all kinds of different things.

Susan: Tell me more of the Tracey story. You went over there the next day...

Melanie: I walk in the door and she pretty much throws me up against the wall and starts kissing me. And I'm thinking, "This is my fucking dream come true. This is just like I always wanted." Then we just went at it. I don't think we got out of bed for hours. She was very intense, into biting and scratching, pleasure/pain stuff. This was not the first time I had considered S/M but it was the first time I had done it. Our relationship progressed into a master/slave type of relationship pretty readily. And I was totally, totally ready for it. I had done my homework, read magazines and books about S/M stuff. I knew what I wanted. And here was this girl, giving it to me, lots of it. It was really scary, I remember each step of the way was really scary.

Susan: When you say you knew what you wanted, what did you want?

Melanie: I wanted fierce raw sex. That definitely meant we were going to play with dildos and do penetration stuff, and I wanted that to be hard and dangerous, like bordering that edge of pain. And I knew I wanted to feel other sensations simultaneously, like I wanted her to hit me. That was freaky to me. I spent a long time not being ready to say I wanted that. And she didn't do it until I was able to ask for it.

Susan: You wanted her to hit you where?

Melanie: My face. And my back. We started playing with things like belts, and it was the same thing; I had to ask for what I wanted. Then I wanted her to leave marks. And at the same time she would be saying things like, "I want to hit you." "I want to hurt you." "I want to leave this mark."

I was very driven by wanting to please her and satisfy her and do what she said. It was very sexy for me to be told what to do. I liked dating someone who had a clear vision of what they wanted and laid it out so I knew exactly what to do to make her happy and to make her pleased, and I felt like I got rewarded by her praise and rewarded by her fucking me.

Susan: Can you tell me about an intense scene?

Melanie: Something would provoke it. Like she'd look at me in a certain way, and I'd look back coyly, and she'd say, "Get on your knees." If she was wearing her strap-on dildo, she might make me suck it. Then inevitably I ended up having to take off my clothing or parts of my clothing and go lie on the bed, and I would get hit with a belt, and she'd make me say I wanted it. She'd hit me on my shoulders and on my back. I could take a lot on my back, and she liked that because she's really strong and always wanted me to wear her out.

Usually I ended up saying my safe word because it would become too much for me.

I remember feeling so proud of myself the time that I got beyond crying. Crying has always been something I don't feel comfortable doing. So being able to cry is profound, a huge release, very transformative. It's always been more of a release for me than orgasm. So I started to cry, but then I got beyond crying, and she continued to beat me, and it was ecstatic.

I hated being hit on my butt, I hated that more than anything. Sometimes I got that, but I didn't like it. I liked being hit in the face a lot. And I loved getting marks, being marked with bruises. It made it last for me, it made the high last.

Eventually Melanie and Tracey broke up — "It was a very ugly, miserable thing," she says — and Melanie spent some time in New York City experimenting to see if she enjoyed S/M activity independent of her relationship with Tracey. She went to a sex club alone one night.

Susan: That strikes me as very nervy.
Melanie: I've always been like that. Sometimes I just get wild hairs up my butt and have to go do these incredibly foxy, dangerous, sexy, spooky things all by myself.

The club was all women, some walking around naked, some clothed. There were shows, safe-sex shows and strippers and belly dancers. And there were rooms for group sex and rooms for private sex and just all kinds of shit going on all over the place.

I met this woman Annette — well, I didn't meet her exactly — I saw her butch self walking around carrying a flashlight. I had this little fetish about flashlights because Tracey had fucked me once with one, and I thought it was the sexiest thing in the world. Eventually I went over to her and said, "What do you do with the flashlight?" We ended up going off into a corner and having this little S/M scene right in the middle of the sex club. She had this huge bag of tricks, paddles and electric shock things and all kinds of weird S/M fetishy toys and clothespins and stuff.

I don't remember what all we did, but I remember we played with her little electric shock gun; that was really cool. It's a little zapper, a low-current electric shock. I was wearing these tall boots, and she zapped it on my boots. It wasn't painful, just startling. Kinda warm. And she had a Ping-Pong paddle with sandpaper on one side. And a spatula. And clothespins. She was very down-to-earth, total working-class S/M stuff. I don't think she had a single thing that cost more than a dollar; everything was a household utensil.

Now, a couple of years after her breakup with Tracey, Melanie has found a new partner, a woman with whom she enjoys both S/M play and other kinds of sex. She has also branched out into new-to-her variations of intense sexual play.

Melanie: I feel like I've always been a bottom — the

person on the receiving end of S/M play — and I am a bottom in my heart, and I think I'm a really good bottom, although I'm a little out of practice. But I've been topping lately. When I'm topping I'm very, very controlling. I am nurturing and maternal and knowledgeable, but at the same time I am Queen Bitch, I just want to be served. Topping has given me a huge respect for tops because it's exhausting, the amount of energy it takes to be responsible for your own pleasure and satisfaction and the well-being of another person's body and psyche is profound. It takes incredible physical endurance as well as emotional maturity, and it takes some mind reading.

My partner, Joan, and I do scenes together, like a mistress/boy scene, which is about her being a boy and giving me, the mistress, sexual pleasure. She and I together have had bottoms that we have co-topped. There was one young woman we saw for six months, and we're seeing another woman now. We tend to beat the poor thing up and then fuck her, which, you know, bottoms love. And come back for more. But most of the sex we have has been more traditional sex with a little bit of roughness thrown in.

Susan: What's the most unconventional thing you like to do sexually that isn't S/M?

Melanie: Probably fucking each other in the butt with dildos. It feels really good, and it's so totally naughty. It amazes me that I can put my gloved finger in her butt, and put another gloved finger in her pussy and can feel my fingers together. It's like I'm having my own little party in there.

I'm also a big sensation slut. I like lots of sensations all at once, all over the place. I want something in my butt, and something in my pussy, and something on my clit, and something on my tits, and then be spanked and have my face hit ... I just want it all at the same time.

Joan and I have really good compatible sex; we're very

good at pleasuring each other. And it's always different, different times of day, different places, different positions, weird toys. It doesn't have that kind of routine that sex can fall into.

Susan: Do you fantasize too?

Melanie: Yes. Sometimes when I close my eyes — this happens with penetrative sex, fisting or some kinds of butt sex, rarely with oral sex — it's like my tongue swells and contracts and fills my whole mouth, and I start to see shapes, black and white things getting bigger and smaller, and angles and curves and hippopotamuses and stars. When I see all these things, it's the biggest high. But that's a sex thing; I don't get the images doing S/M.

Melanie has helped organize several popular women's sex parties, called "raves." I asked her to tell me what they're like.

Melanie: We put on this great big party for women where we had dancers in cages, and pop, and lots of music, and little sex rooms you could go into. It was really fun, really cool. There was lots and lots of Saran Wrap and gloves and condoms, so it was a safe-sex environment. There were lap dancers — strippers who'll come over and do a little dance in your lap — and S/M demonstrations, and fucking demos and masturbation demos, all kinds of stuff. About five hundred women showed up, the oldest the sixty-year-old mother of a friend of mine, and the youngest would be fifteen, if we'd let them in. There was a pretty good representation from ethnic groups, and the full range of sexual interests, from vanilla — standard lesbian sex — to hard-core kinky S/M. Of course the women who come have a certain comfort with a bit of exhibitionism, a little kinky sexy edge to them. We're not talking sexually conservative women.

Susan: You mentioned safe-sex supplies at the rave. What are you observing about lesbians and safe sex? Are they doing safe sex? Are they worrying about safe sex?

Melanie: I think they're worrying about it. A lot of them are talking about it, but most of them aren't doing it consistently. Some of them are doing it some of the time.

Joan and I did the whole thing, for the first six months we were dating, until we had gotten our AIDS and other STD tests twice.

Susan: Would you describe a sex scene using safe sex?

Melanie: The thing I like about safe sex is gloves. And I like lubricant too. The best lubricant is a 50/50 mix of aloe vera gel and Astroglide. Lesbians have this thing about wetness, that if you're wet you're turned on, and if you're not wet, you're not turned on. It usually takes me a little while to start flowing, so I like lube because it takes away that anxiety, that pressure.

The nice thing about gloves is that it lets go some of the taboo about touching people's butts, like it's okay to touch butt because you've got a glove on and you're not worried about poop getting in your fingernails. And of course gloves protect you if you have any cuts and scratches on your hands where the HIV virus could enter.

Now in terms of going down on women and using latex, dental dams are a complete waste of time. Saran Wrap is the total killer thing to use as long as it's non-microwavable; you don't want the microwavable kind because it has porous holes in it. You can make a diaper on your girlfriend out of your Saran Wrap and say, "All right, honey, this is your kinky underwear for the night," and go at it.

I think one of the most important things about safe sex is having a sense of humor, being able to laugh at how ridiculous it is, and just totally going at it with enthusiasm. The first couple of times women use latex together they have to say stuff like, "I know this is really cheesy, but can you feel it when I do this?" and "What does it feel like when I do that?" and "Is that your clit?" Of course, if you're not on that level of communication with your partner, you probably shouldn't be fucking anyway.

Susan: Tell me about being a stripper.

Melanie: I work three hours a week at a peep show. Five dancers at a time are on a stage. The customers go into a little booth, put a quarter in, the window goes up, and they can see the dancers. There are also booths where a microphone goes on and one dancer and the customer talk. It's this mutual masturbation show where she is expected to get him all hot and heavy, he masturbates and tries to come, and she talks with him. She may masturbate or not, depending on what his fantasy is and what she's willing to do and how much he pays her.

I've been on the payroll at this club for about three years. I started working there when I started dating Tracey, to earn extra money. She was patrolling on the weekends, and I went to work. I could make three or four hundred dollars in a weekend.

Susan: Do women ever come to these places?

Melanie: My girlfriend comes to see me. It's real fun, because I have characters I play when I'm dancing, but when I see her, I'll start to laugh and make funny faces at her.

Being a stripper is an amazing expression of erotic potential, and it's a job, just a job that people do. My theory is that every job is prostitution, like being a secretary is really fucking prostitution. Sitting behind a desk without a window, typing all day long for somebody else, wasting paper, getting carpal tunnel syndrome. Prostitution is really an exchange of your body for somebody else's money. Sex work is just more direct than, for instance, secretarial work.

I'm not advocating the health of the sex industry, because it's certainly a dysfunctional, fucked up, mafioso-run industry. But it has also served many marginalized women in many positive ways. It's an important way that women get through their lives. They can earn in twenty hours a week what it would take them forty hours to earn doing something else.

Susan: Do you think of yourself now as bisexual, or as a lesbian, or how do you define your identity?

Melanie: As a dyke.

Susan: What's the difference between a lesbian and a dyke?

Melanie: Right now I'm in a lesbian relationship, and I feel really content and happy, so it's kind of hard to think of any relationship outside of this. But I don't rule out ever sleeping with men again, so I don't feel it's really fair to call myself a lesbian. And some of the fantasies that I have have to do with fucking men, which I think is a very dyke-oriented kind of fantasy.

What "dyke" means to me is that it's okay to talk about and fantasize about all kinds of weird sexual things and not feel like it's against the rules. Being a dyke rather than a lesbian is like saying I'm queer instead of saying I'm homosexual. Being a dyke and being a stripper both make me queer.

Susan: Because why?

Melanie: Because they're perverted and twisted and weird and not normal and not mainstream. They're naughty, and I like naughty things.

Jane

"I really think there's more to sex
than having an orgasm."

My high school boyfriend never forced me to do anything, but I felt uncomfortable a lot; I felt pressured by him. I was right in the middle of a lot of insecurity and not knowing how to deal with all of this sex stuff. Originally I think I wanted to be his girlfriend because it seemed like the right thing to do and I wanted to figure things out. But I was really just putting away my feelings toward girls, trying to shove those in the back of my mind somewhere. And that wasn't working because I was having dreams about women.

The first dream I had about a girl was about my friend Maria. I dreamed about us sleeping in the same bed and holding each other. It was very scary for me because I felt like, What if somebody finds out I'm having this dream? What if *she* finds out I'm having this dream? But there were also really wonderful feelings, sexual feelings, even if the dreams themselves weren't sexual. Sometimes I think that I felt more like my real self when I was dreaming than when I was awake.

I am talking with Jane the day before her nineteenth birthday. I have picked her up at her mother's house in a middle-class suburb of Charlotte, North Carolina, and we have driven to a nearby park. We are sitting across from each other at a picnic table, surrounded by rhododendron bushes that protect us from other people who are using the park on this midweek spring morning.

Jane is a young woman with short blonde hair, neatly and modishly dressed in a black leather jacket and jeans, a uniform that simultaneously announces her youthful lesbian identity and wards off the April breeze. Not a line creases her face, yet she projects maturity and solidity, partly through her size and partly through her careful thoughtfulness. She pauses frequently during the interview, furrowing her brow, looking into the middle distance, comfortable with the silence that passes while she considers her answers.

Susan: Would you say you are lesbian or gay or . . . ?
Jane: I would say that I identify as lesbian, but I do not exclude the possibility of changing my identity at some point in the future. Sometimes the words that people put on themselves hurt them. They put you into this role of

what you have to be and what the rules are for being this. I don't think that's good for people.

Susan: Tell me some more about your boyfriend and how you came to identify as lesbian, even if only for the time being.

Jane: Jim and I were together for a year and three months, beginning when I started high school at age fifteen. He was my first significant relationship, which means to me that I put a good deal of myself into the relationship and changed because of it. It started off more as friendly than anything else, then after a while we started kissing and making out. We never actually had penetrative sex, but we got real close to it. He had this little playhouse next to his house. We would go in there and mess around. One day we were getting to the point of having sex, he went into the house to get a condom, and his parents came home unexpectedly. So there I was hiding and putting on my clothes and . . . [Jane laughs.] Looking back it seems very comedic, but at the time it was traumatic.

That was a Friday, and I didn't see him until the next Monday. That weekend he went away on a retreat with his church and came back a born-again Christian. Now he wanted to have a platonic relationship, which was kind of convenient for me because right that same weekend I was having these feelings like, gosh, I might not be following my heart here, this might not be the best thing for me. I was relieved almost.

At the time I thought a lot about women's skin as opposed to men's skin because Jim had this skin that was . . . it wasn't soft. It didn't feel the way I wanted it to feel. He wasn't as soft and cuddly as women are. I'd think a lot about cuddling up to women's breasts, or just touching a woman's neck. That's as far as my thoughts or dreams went sexually.

Jim and I always had very different opinions on the gay issue. My opinion was that there was no problem at all, gays were just like everybody else. He thought gays were going to hell, he was very vehement about it. On this one day — I don't even know where this came from — I told him that I thought I was bisexual. It just came out of my mouth, and then afterward I thought, Uh oh, that was a bad idea. [Jane is laughing.] So the first person I came out to was my boyfriend, but I came out as bisexual, of course.

Jim and I got on the bus, and at first he was not holding my hand or putting his arm around me. Then we got off at a park near my house, and he started kissing me and fondling me. I started crying because I didn't know what was going on; I didn't like it at all. Then he stopped and told me he was breaking up with me. I think he felt really threatened by my saying that I was bisexual, because earlier, when we were just friends, he had talked about having the same feelings for guys that I was having for girls.

So then I wasn't involved with anyone for six months. I was really depressed at first that Jim and I had broken up, but it wore off a lot faster than I thought it would. I had time to sort things out a little. And, since I wasn't just focused on Jim, I found some friends. And from there I realized that I was not bisexual but that I was a lesbian and so . . .

Susan: How did you realize this?

Jane: That's a good question. I don't know. [She thinks quietly for a few moments.] At that point in my life I was dealing with my parents' divorce, and I was letting all my feelings come back up, and kind of clearing them out and sorting them. But I don't know how I came to the conclusion that I was lesbian.

I went to the library and read books about gay people,

like Rita Mae Brown. I looked through the card catalogue under "gay," which said, "See homosexuality," which, when I looked it up, was a study of deviants. You had to ask the desk to ask the librarian to get the book for you, so that didn't sound like too great an option. I read a paperback for gay youth that had little stick people with pink triangles on them. I don't really know how I got to the point of figuring out my sexuality.

Susan: Once you'd figured it out, did you do anything about it?

Jane: I told my sister.

Susan: How old were you?

Jane: I was sixteen. I told her what had happened with Jim, and that I thought I was gay. She wasn't too shocked. It felt to me like she already knew, in a way.

The next person I came out to was my gay friend Max at school. And he was so happy, he was just thrilled. He was jumping around and saying "That's wonderful!" and, "Now I have someone to be gay with." It was such a great experience coming out to him, because I had thought it was a terrible thing that I was gay; I was just really sad about it. I felt like my world was going to end somehow.

Susan: What was sad for you about it?

Jane: I thought of it as a tragedy, because being gay had never been presented to me in a positive light before. I thought I would never be happy, that gays went to bars and rode motorcycles and were alone. The number one thing I thought about being gay was that I was going to end up alone, because I wouldn't be married and I wouldn't get to have kids. That's what scared me the most. I was very ignorant on the gay thing.

I had thought that once Jim and my sister and Max knew, that was too many already; I wasn't coming out to anyone else as long as I lived. Then the next week Max and I came out in high school together, and I came out to my whole family plus my grandparents plus everyone. I wanted to teach everyone in the whole world what being gay is about and, you know, why gays are cool.

Susan: How did you go from thinking being gay was a terrible tragedy to thinking it was such a wonderful thing that you wanted to tell everybody?

Jane: Basically, it was Max; he was my savior. It took me forever to come out to him. I mean, I told him I wanted to talk to him about something, and two weeks later I finally got up the nerve. I'm so glad I came out to him. He took me home, I cried, he brought me books, he brought me a copy of *The Advocate.* He took me to a drop-in center that has food and housing and counseling and all sorts of stuff for gay and lesbian youth.

My coming out experience with my mom, though, was really bad. I'd talked to Max's mom, who said, "Well, you know, if your mom wants to call me, we can talk about things." I got a brochure from P-FLAG, Parents and Friends of Lesbians and Gays. I made a nice dinner and sat her down and said I had something important I needed to tell her, that I was a lesbian. She laughed at me — to put me down, you know — which was like the worst thing she could have done. The point we're at now, she's wonderfully supportive. I mean, she's really great. But for a while things were really hard.

Anyway, Max and I came out publicly at school. We were so out people would know we were gay, but didn't know our first names. We started the first student-initiated gay/lesbian/bisexual support group in a Charlotte high school. Then prom time came around. I got this threat message in my locker that if I came to the prom with a girl, whoever it was was going to beat me up. But I wasn't really concerned about it.

I went to the prom with my girlfriend, Greta. We both wore tuxes. Greta and I were never very mushy, so we didn't really kiss too much or anything, but we were holding hands and dancing. And that was my last high-school experience.

The interesting thing is that coming out in high school suddenly sprung me into the popular crowd. I had never before been popular, I rarely had friends, just Jim, so when I came out, people at least knew who I was. People kind of respected me.

Jane had taken her girlfriend Greta to the prom, but her principal romantic interest at the time was Madeleine, her first woman lover and her current partner. They met at the gay and lesbian drop-in center, when Jane was seventeen. Maddy and Jane now live together in Jane's separate space in the basement of her mother's house.

Jane: Maddy is a really wonderful person. She is the first person I had sex with, like really. Well, I had sex with Jim too, at least I had oral sex on him. He never had oral sex with me. But Maddy was the first person that I really enjoyed a sexual experience with where another person was involved.

Susan: Are you saying that you had enjoyed sex with yourself?

Jane: Oh, I'm an avid masturbator! I remember when I was about ten years old I was going through cupboards in the bathroom — I was a very curious little kid, I liked to open things up and sort through stuff and look in places that I wasn't supposed to look — anyway, I found what I now realize were tampons. I brought one over to my mom and asked, "What is this?" and she told me what it was and what it was for. So I took it up into my bedroom and tried it out. That was my first experience of sexual feelings that I can remember. It started out as scientific curiosity, but it turned into being very sexy.

Susan: How important is masturbating to you now?

Jane: I don't masturbate as often anymore because now

I live with my girlfriend, and she gets kind of offended if I masturbate and she's around. She doesn't masturbate at all. I think she's kind of uncomfortable with the whole thing; I think she feels threatened by it, actually.

I see masturbation as not just a sexual thing, but also a way of figuring yourself out. I think it's good, a really healthy thing to do. I probably masturbate once a week now, but before I was masturbating every other day.

Susan: What would you do?

Jane: Well, I have a bedroom in the basement of my mom's house, with my own couch and bathroom and everything. It was private. So, back when I was masturbating a lot, I might lie on my stomach on my bed and read something that I thought was interesting and would get me feeling sexy. I remember reading in *The Hite Report* about masturbation and orgasms and all of this really interesting stuff. So I would try things out. I would maybe kiss my hand or rub my arm and touch my breasts, and then touch my vagina. I never really did penetration, but I did like playing with the opening of my vagina. I've played with my anus. And I really liked touching my clitoris a lot.

A lot of my sexual experiences with Jim felt negative emotionally, and they weren't really physically exciting to me either. I enjoyed touching myself a lot better than I liked being touched by someone else. I didn't even know if I wanted anyone else to touch me. And so masturbating was my chance to relax and really enjoy my body. I never had an orgasm from masturbation, though, until after I'd had an orgasm during sex with Maddy. Of course, I really think there's more to sex than having an orgasm.

Susan: So tell me about sex with Madeleine.

Jane: I remember the very first time that we had sex she was gentle and loving toward me, she would ask me, "Does this feel good?" "Is this okay?" "How are you feeling?" before she would try anything else. It made me feel safe, which was a feeling I hadn't had sexually, except with myself.

Susan: Would you describe this first time for me? Like where you were and what happened, who did what to whom?

Jane: I can't. [Her fair cheeks blush.] I'm getting nervous.

Susan: That's all right. [I wait, but just a few seconds go by.]

Jane: One of the things I liked best about Maddy was that on our very first date she brought me this rune. [Jane fishes in her pocket and pulls out a small square object imprinted with some hieroglyphic symbol.] It's an Irish rune that means growth, rebirth, and new beginnings. She gave it to me right out in the middle of the Park Road Shopping Center, which I really liked. Maddy's twenty-two and is very out. I really respected that, it was exciting for me.

So, anyway, we were on the couch in her apartment, kissing and making out. She was touching my breasts and stuff. She said, "If we keep doing this we're going to end up going farther." And I said, "That's okay." So she took my hand and walked me into the bedroom. At this point I was thinking, I didn't know we were going to go *this* far [Jane laughs] and she sat me down on the floor and said, "I want to show you something." Then — this is the coolest part — she took off her shirt with one swipe of her arm. I just thought it was so suave. It was really great, real exciting.

Then I was kissing her breasts and sucking on them and touching her. She laid me back on the floor, and first we started just kind of dry humping, and then she took off my pants and started touching me. She touched my clitoris and touched my vagina and stroked me all over the place. We didn't have oral sex, just fingers, and it was really nice. The sad part is that half an hour later she had to go to work, so we didn't get to hang out for the rest of the day and spend time with each other. That's the only thing that I regret.

Susan: Did you touch her too?

Jane: Not that time. It was probably a month before she let me touch her. She's very, very sensitive about her body because she's had a lot of sexual abuse, really scary, bad stuff. With previous sexual partners she hasn't let most of them touch her at all. So I remember the first time she let me touch her, it was really a privilege, you know.

Susan: How did your first orgasm come to pass?

Jane: I'll have to think when that was [long pause]. I'm not even clear when my very first orgasm was, because at the time I thought maybe it was an orgasm, but I wasn't sure, so I was going to wait and see if I had another one.

Then when I finally did realize that I was having an orgasm, the thing that stands out most clearly in my mind is that Maddy felt like she had accomplished something. She wanted all the details because she'd never had an orgasm. I felt kind of awkward answering questions about my first orgasm since I didn't feel like I was really an expert at that point.

Susan: How did it feel? Can you describe it?

Jane: Well . . . when I get close to having an orgasm, I have a lot of shaking. I'm earthquaking all over the place, bouncing around, especially here [she points to her pelvis]. My feet are shaking all over. Then when I'm getting right up to the point of orgasm I have to have something to hold on to, like Maddy, or if we're having oral sex and she's down there, I'll hold on to the bed.

But that's not saying how it feels. I'm trying to think. [Jane wrinkles up her brow and squints her eyes with the effort.] Something is boiling. It feels like all of this warm stuff is gurgling up and getting ready to explode, and then it happens, and all of a sudden I'm warm and soft and fuzzy all over. One of the things I've noticed with having orgasms is that I think I feel more in touch with my body at that moment than any other time because I can feel every last millimeter of my skin everywhere, I can feel touches everywhere all at once.

Then, after I have an orgasm, Maddy has to stay and stroke me and hold me. That's crucial to me. I won't have sex unless I'm going to have some time afterward.

Susan: How did it happen that Maddy let you make love to her?

Jane: During the process of our getting together we had broken up two or three times. When I first met Maddy she had been clean and sober only two months. Her whole life was inconsistent and still mostly is. In the year and four months we've been together she's lived in eight different places and worked five or six different jobs. So we'd broken up, and she had a girlfriend, and I had a girlfriend, Greta, the girl I took to the senior prom. And Maddy knew that Greta was letting me touch her. Maddy started feeling very uncomfortable with that; I think that made her jealous.

Eventually Greta and I broke up, and Maddy and Carol broke up. Then one day Maddy and I went for a walk, and she told me she loved me, that she was in love with me, and that she wanted to be with me and she didn't want to play any more games and that she wanted to let me touch her.

I took some time to think. I had a lot of hurt feelings because of all the breaking up, and I didn't want to go through it again. But, luckily, things have turned out fine. We've never even gotten close to breaking up since then. She's gaining some consistency in her life, and she's a lot better talking about feelings and not just things. She's just the most beautiful person I've ever known. I'm totally in love with her.

Susan: So did you get to make love to her?

Jane: Yes, about two weeks later, which was the first time we'd made love after getting back together. It was an afternoon. I like making love during the daylight, especially with windows open. Maddy's apartment had an alcove that was a semidome, with these tall windows that surrounded her bed. We were lying in bed with each other, naked, with the sun shining on us, kissing and stuff. I said, "Would it be all right if I touch you?" And she said, "Yeah, that would be wonderful." So I had oral sex with her. She feels more comfortable with oral sex than with fingers. It was really nice.

Usually when we make love, we spend a long time at it. I think the first time we had sex it was only an hour, but that's probably the shortest amount of time we've ever spent. So this time we spent probably about three hours. Foreplay is a big part of it for us. We like to start off just kissing, and then we stroke each other and hold each other and kiss every part of each other's bodies.

Susan: Would you talk to each other?

Jane: We do some talking, but for the most part, no. One of the things I really like her doing to me is kissing right here [she rolls to her side and touches herself], where your leg and your hip meet. The main point is "worship of the body," that's my term for it. Just making sure that every little piece of her body or my body is getting touched and loved.

Susan: What's your favorite thing to do sexually, if you had to pick one thing?

Jane: To have oral sex with her, to do oral sex on her. That's my favorite thing to do, probably because that's the least explored aspect of sex for us. When she asks me to do that, it just makes me feel wonderful. It's not just the physical side of it; it's also the emotional side of it. Limiting sex to the actual sex act — like oral sex, or digital sex — is a terrible thing to do because sex is the whole experience. A lot of times when we're making love we will do a lot of different things because we take some time. So we'll start out with her eating me out, and then we'll go from there to anal sex, or . . . I don't know, we'll just do all sorts of things. It's from the very beginning — just starting off kissing — to the very end. That's the sex experience for me.

Susan: Do you like to have sexual fantasies?

Jane: Yeah, but most of them are realistic; I'm a very practical person. The only fantasy that sounds really great to me has to do with having been raised Catholic. The cathedral is such a beautiful place, so the idea of being in a huge cathedral with light coming through all those stained glass windows and — this is going to sound sacrilegious — making love on the altar. I don't mean it in a sacrilegious way; I just mean that would be so beautiful to me. I think making love with a woman is the most wonderful thing in the world, a beautiful, wonderful thing. So the idea of offering that up to something greater is really inspiration to me. That would be my fantasy.

Most of my fantasies are about places rather than about how and which way, that sort of thing. I would love to make love with Madeleine down at the ocean, at night, with the surf. Of course it would be totally cold, sand all over the place, but the concept is really nice. And besides, these are fantasies; they don't have to be realistic. I have to remind myself of that all the time.

Susan: Can you think of a time that you've had sex that something funny happened?

Jane: Oh yeah. [She laughs.] We got a strap-on recently, because we like trying out new things. I think it's supposed to be a G-spot one, and the whole thing was pretty expensive. It's purple, and the harness is black leather. We were thinking about doing red leather, but the red and the violet combination wouldn't look so good.

Anyway, earlier we had had this idealistic lesbian

theory that if you're going to be a lesbian, you don't need a penis — not even a plastic one — and we didn't want any of that stuff. So we were kind of closeted about our strap-on for a while. We told ourselves that the reason we wanted to get it was that it would be really nice to have our hands free to do whatever we wanted.

So, back to the funny part. I had a meeting that evening, so I was quickly running home to try it out. Now those things can be really awkward, and we couldn't get it to work at first. Madeliene strapped it on, but aiming the thing wasn't working; it kept slipping out of me. Maddy was getting more and more frustrated; she was kind of angry about it. But I thought it was funny because I had been so nervous about the whole, you know, fake penis thing. So I was laughing hysterically the whole time. Finally we got it working, but then it fell out again, and I had a huge pussy fart, a big wailing one, and we both started laughing. And that was the end of that.

Since then I think we've only tried it out two other times. One of those times it worked just fine, and we had a wonderful time. I'm not into penetration that often, and Maddy's not into penetration at all. And even when I am into penetration, for the most part I prefer hands because they're not cold. And they just feel better to me; they're not lifeless. But more than anything else, we got it for an experiment anyway, just to try it out.

Susan: Have you done other things as experiments?

Jane: We've tried anal sex, with fingers. And we've done fisting. Actually, even though I don't like penetration, I really like fisting. But I have to be in the mood for it.

Susan: Can Maddy get her whole hand inside you?

Jane: Mmmhmm. [She's nodding, yes.] She has big hands too. But we have to work up to it.

Susan: How do you work up to it?

Jane: One finger at a time. [We both laugh so loudly that we catch the attention of a passing walker. We hunch up closer to each other, making sure we're not being overheard.]

Susan: What do you think is the key to making fisting work?

Jane: Being very relaxed with your partner, very comfortable, and staying in communication with each other, talking the whole thing out while you're doing it. Maddy is great about communication in bed. That's one of her best qualities. I can't understand anyone having good sex with someone they just met. That just doesn't make sense to me at all, because Maddy and I have had to really work into good sex.

Sex is a lot of work; number one, making sure both of you are feeling safe and comfortable, and, number two, that you're doing things both of you can enjoy at the same time. It's complicated stuff.

Susan: So Maddy would talk to you while she is fisting you?

Jane: Yeah. I'd be lying on my back, and we'd start off with just two fingers. Then she'd say, "I'm going to put in another finger. Is that okay?" Then after a while she'd say, "Now I've got four fingers in you. How are you feeling?" Of course, we'd be using major amounts of lubrication too. I like water-based lubricant way better than oil-based.

The whole time she would be doing something else too, like touching my breast or stroking my face. It helps to be a bit distracted because you have to be really relaxed. I think we do fisting too just for the experience, which is fine.

Susan: Would you have an orgasm fisting?

Jane: No. But it's really exciting to feel someone's

whole hand inside of you. First of all, the concept is really exciting, but also just the feeling of being that filled. I don't know how to put it . . . I feel almost dizzy, feverish. It sounds negative, but it's exciting.

I've ejaculated before too, and that's the feeling I usually get right before I ejaculate. I feel like I'm going to faint, like I'm wavering between reality and . . . the subconscious. It's weird, hard to describe.

Susan: How do you feel about anal sex?

Jane: [Long pause.] I think the excitement in it for me is more the taboo of it. It's not really that exciting for me sexually. [She pauses again, searching for something more exciting to tell me about.] We've done a little bit of role playing, but that doesn't make me feel safe.

Susan: What do you mean, role playing?

Jane: You know, dominance-submission stuff.

Susan: Who is which?

Jane: She's the dominant, of course. I don't think she'd feel comfortable at all being submissive. It's hard enough for her to feel comfortable being submissive in real life. I prefer, though, not to consider myself top or bottom, butch or femme.

Susan: Does one of you initiate sex more than the other?

Jane: At the beginning of things, Maddy was, because I was being kind of passive. But now I'm definitely the one who starts things more often. If you had to put roles onto us, she'd be the top and I'd be the bottom. The nice thing about being a bottom is that you have all the power. The top is taking the active role, but as far as all of the emotional aspects go, and when we're going to have sex, and how we're going to have sex, the bottom has all the power. Because if the bottom isn't interested, the top can't do anything. Especially since this particular top does not masturbate whatsoever. So she has to make some effort to make it nice, because if I'm not interested, then there she is . . . alone and horny.

Susan: Do you think the way you are sexually is reflected in your relationship as a whole?

Jane: I think that our relationship and our sexual relationship are very different. They're definitely connected, but I think we are on much more equal territory in our relationship. I sometimes feel frustrated with our sex life because the thing I enjoy most is getting to make love with her. I get frustrated sometimes because we'll go for maybe a month before she'll let me make love to her. That hurts my feelings in a way. Of course I know that if it was just her heart that was involved, she would let me make love to her whenever I wanted to, but she has all these bad feelings that come up. And sometimes when I make love to her she zones out, which makes me feel sad. So it's a very delicate matter. I want to be able to make love to her, but I don't want to make her unhappy. [Jane pauses and looks away from me for a moment.] I have some of that stuff too.

Susan: That sexual abuse stuff?

Jane: Yeah, I've been sexually abused. I'm still in the process of dealing with it, so I can't really talk about it. But it comes out in different ways with me. When I'm being penetrated by fingers or a dildo or whatever, I need to be able to feel at the same time like I'm in control of the situation. I need to feel safe. If I get feeling very unsafe, I'll start crying. So it's the same delicate situation with me. Except that the other thing about penetration is that sometimes when Maddy is putting her fingers inside of me I feel like I'm being lifted up by that somehow. It's almost like feeling a power. It's feeling like . . . I don't know . . . It's really great sometimes.

Jane and I sit quietly for a while, acknowledging the

difficult situation she and Maddy must deal with, absorbing the reality of how complex sexuality can be. We look away from each other, focusing on a nearby robin busily tugging on a worm. Soon the robin hops away, worm in beak. Jane takes a deep breath and looks at me again.

Susan: What do you think is the importance of sex to the rest of your life? I'm trying to get at what you think sex means for you.

Jane: That's a really good question. I've never thought about that at all. Well... it's taken me some time to feel comfortable having sex at all. Letting another person be like that with you is a big deal, especially if you've had some sexual abuse or anything like that. Even if you haven't. So I feel proud of having sex now. I feel like sex with Maddy is the most wonderful thing in the whole world because it's my first real experience of pleasurable sex with another person. I'm in a euphoric state about it.

And in terms of our relationship — in terms of any romantic relationship — I think sex is a very important thing. Being able to physically express how much you care about another person is something special. It's amazing to me how you can do that, how bodies can work together like that. I mean, it's amazing and beautiful. I love sex. I admit it freely!

But I don't believe that to be a lesbian you have to have sex. I don't want people to think that in order to be gay they have to go out and screw somebody. I thought that was true when I was first coming out, and that restricted my understanding of the joy of being a lesbian. Being a lesbian is about your feelings, and not only your feelings for other women, but your feelings for yourself.

The word "lesbian" no longer means to me a person who has sex with other women. It means more. It's a culmination of my experiences, my coming out at school and to my family, my first kiss with a woman, being part of the gay political movement, all that stuff, all of those wonderful experiences and the scary experiences too.

Like the dreams I had when I was a little kid, that's part of me being a lesbian. Coming out to my mom and having her laugh at me. Those sorts of things make me more of a lesbian than just me having sex with a woman, because identity is not something that you can make with your body. Identity is something that comes out of your soul.

Let's Talk About Sex:
Some Guidelines

I asked the following questions of the women I interviewed for this book. It is my hope that these questions will help you reflect upon your own sexuality and talk more openly with your partner or with friends. Here are some guidelines you may want to follow to make the process safer, more fruitful, and more fun:

• There are *no right or wrong answers* to any of these questions; the challenge is to be honest with yourself, to examine your heart, and then to tell the truth about yourself to your partner or friends. Do not judge yourself.

• *Talk only about yourself* — about how you feel, what you are experiencing, what you want — not for or about your partner or the other women in your discussion group. Do not speak for or judge your friends.

• *Keep yourself safe.* Push yourself to take risks, but do not go into territory that does not feel emotionally safe, that is unexplored and potentially dangerous. Some sexual issues — like incest, for example — may be more safely discussed with professional help.

• *Do not be put off* by the somewhat academic-sounding nature of the questions. The questions may be boring, but your answers will be dynamite!

• Choose *just a few questions* to discuss in any one get-together, so you have time for everyone to talk in some depth. Then, if you liked the experience, meet again and move on to other questions.

• These questions are never meant to be answered with a simple yes or no, even though they are sometimes phrased that way. *Give as complete answers as you can,* taking into account, of course, how many women are in your group and how much time you have for any particular session.

• *Talk in as much graphic detail* as you can manage. This way everyone can understand exactly what you mean — and can get practical tips as well!

• *Have fun.* This is supposed to be an interesting and revealing experience, but also entertaining and fun . . . and sexy. If things get too heavy, take a break, move on to another person, pick another subject to discuss.

Good luck!

THE QUESTIONS

1. What was your family like about sex? What did you

learn from them that you feel affects how you are about sex today?

2. Have you had any sexual experience with boys/men? What was this like? How have these experiences contributed to your sexual life as a lesbian?

3. When did you first become attracted to girls/women? What were the circumstances of this first attraction? What did you feel about it? What did you do about it?

4. When was your first experience with a girl/woman that you consider sexual? Who was she? What happened? What did this experience mean to you about being a lesbian?

5. When did you first think of yourself as lesbian/gay? What were the circumstances around your coming to this decision/realization?

6. Do you think of being lesbian as a choice, or as the way you were born, or as having some other source or cause?

7. How do you define lesbians "having sex"? Is having sex different from being sexual? Is feeling sexual being sexual? Are hugging and kissing being sexual? Do you have to touch genitals to be sexual? Why or why not?

8. What is the relationship between identifying as a lesbian and having sex with women? Do you have to have sex with women in order to define yourself as a lesbian? Want to have sex with a woman? Be currently having sex with a woman? Have sex only with women?

9. What do you most like to do when you're having sex? [Describe this in as much physical detail as you can.] What do you most like her to do for you? What do you most like to do for her?

10. What are your favorite sensitive areas on your body, your favorite places to be touched? What are areas where you don't like to be touched?

11. What are the qualities you like in a lover? What are the qualities you like in yourself as a lover?

12. Looking back over your life as a lesbian, what are some of your favorite sexual encounters, experiences you remember as being particularly fun? exciting? inventive? passionate?

13. What is the funniest thing that's ever happened to you in a sexual situation?

14. What is the most unconventional thing you do sexually? What is it you like about this? What are some other unconventional things you like to do?

15. What is one thing that you are not currently doing sexually that you would like to do? What would you need to do to make this happen?

16. Has your sexual life changed over your years of being a lesbian? What are some of these changes? To what do you attribute these changes?

17. Do you, if you are currently single, or you and your partner, if you are coupled, do anything in a conscious way to enhance your sexual life? What do you do? How does this improve your sexual life?

18. What do you feel is the relationship between being intimate with a person and being sexual with her? Can you be intimate without being sexual? Can you be sexual without being intimate? Does being sexual add some element of intimacy that is otherwise missing?

19. Is it important for you to be monogamous with a woman if you are being sexual with her? If so, how do you define being monogamous? At what point in a relationship does monogamy become important to you? Why is monogamy important? What does monogamy accomplish for your relationship? for your sexual life?

20. Is it important for you to be nonmonogamous with the women with whom you are sexual? If so, how do you define being nonmonogamous? Are there any rules you follow to guide your behavior with multiple sexual

partners? Why is nonmonogamy important to you? How have you been able to combine being sexual with more than one woman at a time?

21. Have you ever been in a sexual relationship with a woman of a race different from your own? Of a social class different from your own? Of a religion different from your own? What were some of the advantages and challenges of these relationships? What was relevant to the sexual part of your relationship about your racial or class or religious differences?

22. Have you ever been in a sexual relationship with a woman who is differently abled than yourself? For example, Who is deaf if you are hearing? Who is hearing if you are deaf? What are the advantages and challenges of these relationships? What was relevant to the sexual part of your relationship about your different physical abilities?

23. Do you like to talk while you're having sex? Do you like to talk after you've had sex? What do you like to talk about? What is the purpose of your talking?

24. Do you enjoy masturbation? What is it about masturbation that is particularly satisfying to you? Is there anything about masturbating that you find unsatisfying?

25. Do you like sexual fantasies? When do you like to have them: Walking around during the day? In your dreams? While you're making love?

26. What is a sexual fantasy you have that you particularly like? [Describe in as much detail as possible.]

27. What do you think is the meaning or point for you of having sexual fantasies, i.e., what do they do for you?

28. What are the differences, if any, between what you fantasize about doing sexually and what you actually do sexually in your real life? Do you have any desire to experience what you fantasize about? If yes, how would you go about making this happen?

29. Do you worry about whether or not what you fantasize doing is normal? Politically correct? Exotic

enough? What is it about this fantasy that makes you uncomfortable? Have you considered ways you could change these feelings of discomfort so you would feel more accepting of your fantasies?

30. Do you enjoy any kinds of sex toys? What kinds? What do they do to enhance your sexual life? Are there any problems you have experienced with their use?

31. What do you consider vanilla or "regular" lesbian sex? [Be as detailed in your description as possible.] Do you enjoy any variations on vanilla sex? What do you most enjoy about this kind of sexual experience?

32. What do you do in your sexual life to protect yourself from HIV/AIDS and other sexually transmitted diseases? How do you feel about what you are doing? Do you feel safe having the sex you are having? What could you do to feel safer?

33. What is the importance of sex to the rest of your life? What does being sexual mean to you? What does being sexual with women mean to you?

And — now that you have completed some part or all of this process — the last question:

34. What has it been like for you to discuss your sexual life with your partner or your friends? What has been most valuable about this experience? What have you learned that has been most important to you? What problems did you encounter? What impact has talking about sex had on your sexual life? Did you have a good time? Would you recommend this experience to your friends?

A few of the publications of
THE NAIAD PRESS, INC.
P.O. Box 10543 • Tallahassee, Florida 32302
Phone (904) 539-5965
Toll-Free Order Number: 1-800-533-1973
Mail orders welcome. Please include 15% postage.
Write or call for our free catalog which also features an
incredible selection of lesbian videos.

INNER CIRCLE by Claire McNab. 208 pp. 8th Carol Ashton
Mystery.   ISBN 1-56280-135-X $10.95

LESBIAN SEX: AN ORAL HISTORY by Susan Johnson.
240 pp. Need we say more?   ISBN 1-56280-142-2   14.95

BABY, IT'S COLD by Jaye Maiman. 256 pp. 5th Robin Miller
Mystery.   ISBN 1-56280-141-4   19.95

WILD THINGS by Karin Kallmaker. 240 pp. By the undisputed
mistress of lesbian romance.   ISBN 1-56280-139-2   10.95

THE GIRL NEXT DOOR by Mindy Kaplan. 208 pp. Just what
you'd expect.   ISBN 1-56280-140-6   10.95

NOW AND THEN by Penny Hayes. 240 pp. Romance on the
westward journey.   ISBN 1-56280-121-X   10.95

HEART ON FIRE by Diana Simmonds. 176 pp. The romantic and
erotic rival of *Curious Wine*.   ISBN 1-56280-152-X   10.95

DEATH AT LAVENDER BAY by Lauren Wright Douglas. 208 pp.
1st Allison O'Neil Mystery.   ISBN 1-56280-085-X   10.95

YES I SAID YES I WILL by Judith McDaniel. 272 pp. Hot
romance by famous author.   ISBN 1-56280-138-4   10.95

FORBIDDEN FIRES by Margaret C. Anderson. Edited by Mathilda
Hills. 176 pp. Famous author's "unpublished" Lesbian romance.
                                                            ISBN 1-56280-123-6   21.95

SIDE TRACKS by Teresa Stores. 160 pp. Gender-bending
Lesbians on the road.   ISBN 1-56280-122-8   10.95

HOODED MURDER by Annette Van Dyke. 176 pp. 1st Jessie
Batelle Mystery.   ISBN 1-56280-134-1   10.95

WILDWOOD FLOWERS by Julia Watts. 208 pp. Hilarious and
heart-warming tale of true love.   ISBN 1-56280-127-9   10.95

NEVER SAY NEVER by Linda Hill. 224 pp. Rule #1: Never get involved
with . . .   ISBN 1-56280-126-0   10.95

THE SEARCH by Melanie McAllester. 240 pp. Exciting top cop
Tenny Mendoza case. ISBN 1-56280-150-3 10.95

THE WISH LIST by Saxon Bennett. 192 pp. Romance through
the years. ISBN 1-56280-125-2 10.95

FIRST IMPRESSIONS by Kate Calloway. 208 pp. P.I. Cassidy
James' first case. ISBN 1-56280-133-3 10.95

OUT OF THE NIGHT by Kris Bruyer. 192 pp. Spine-tingling
thriller. ISBN 1-56280-120-1 10.95

NORTHERN BLUE by Tracey Richardson. 224 pp. Police recruits
Miki & Miranda — passion in the line of fire. ISBN 1-56280-118-X 10.95

LOVE'S HARVEST by Peggy J. Herring. 176 pp. by the author of
Once More With Feeling. ISBN 1-56280-117-1 10.95

THE COLOR OF WINTER by Lisa Shapiro. 208 pp. Romantic
love beyond your wildest dreams. ISBN 1-56280-116-3 10.95

FAMILY SECRETS by Laura DeHart Young. 208 pp. Enthralling
romance and suspense. ISBN 1-56280-119-8 10.95

INLAND PASSAGE by Jane Rule. 288 pp. Tales exploring conven-
tional & unconventional relationships. ISBN 0-930044-56-8 10.95

DOUBLE BLUFF by Claire McNab. 208 pp. 7th Carol Ashton
Mystery. ISBN 1-56280-096-5 10.95

BAR GIRLS by Lauran Hoffman. 176 pp. See the movie, read
the book! ISBN 1-56280-115-5 10.95

THE FIRST TIME EVER edited by Barbara Grier & Christine
Cassidy. 272 pp. Love stories by Naiad Press authors.
ISBN 1-56280-086-8 14.95

MISS PETTIBONE AND MISS McGRAW by Brenda Weathers.
208 pp. A charming ghostly love story. ISBN 1-56280-151-1 10.95

CHANGES by Jackie Calhoun. 208 pp. Involved romance and
relationships. ISBN 1-56280-083-3 10.95

FAIR PLAY by Rose Beecham. 256 pp. 3rd Amanda Valentine
Mystery. ISBN 1-56280-081-7 10.95

PAXTON COURT by Diane Salvatore. 256 pp. Erotic and wickedly
funny contemporary tale about the business of learning to live
together. ISBN 1-56280-109-0 21.95

PAYBACK by Celia Cohen. 176 pp. A gripping thriller of romance,
revenge and betrayal. ISBN 1-56280-084-1 10.95

THE BEACH AFFAIR by Barbara Johnson. 224 pp. Sizzling
summer romance/mystery/intrigue. ISBN 1-56280-090-6 10.95

GETTING THERE by Robbi Sommers. 192 pp. Nobody does it
like Robbi! ISBN 1-56280-099-X 10.95

FINAL CUT by Lisa Haddock. 208 pp. 2nd Carmen Ramirez
Mystery. ISBN 1-56280-088-4 10.95

FLASHPOINT by Katherine V. Forrest. 256 pp. A Lesbian
blockbuster! ISBN 1-56280-079-5   10.95

CLAIRE OF THE MOON by Nicole Conn. Audio Book —Read
by Marianne Hyatt. ISBN 1-56280-113-9   16.95

FOR LOVE AND FOR LIFE: INTIMATE PORTRAITS OF
LESBIAN COUPLES by Susan Johnson. 224 pp.
ISBN 1-56280-091-4   14.95

DEVOTION by Mindy Kaplan. 192 pp. See the movie — read
the book! ISBN 1-56280-093-0   10.95

SOMEONE TO WATCH by Jaye Maiman. 272 pp. 4th Robin
Miller Mystery. ISBN 1-56280-095-7   10.95

GREENER THAN GRASS by Jennifer Fulton. 208 pp. A young
woman — a stranger in her bed. ISBN 1-56280-092-2   10.95

TRAVELS WITH DIANA HUNTER by Regine Sands. Erotic
lesbian romp. Audio Book (2 cassettes) ISBN 1-56280-107-4   16.95

CABIN FEVER by Carol Schmidt. 256 pp. Sizzling suspense
and passion. ISBN 1-56280-089-1   10.95

THERE WILL BE NO GOODBYES by Laura DeHart Young. 192
pp. Romantic love, strength, and friendship. ISBN 1-56280-103-1   10.95

FAULTLINE by Sheila Ortiz Taylor. 144 pp. Joyous comic
lesbian novel. ISBN 1-56280-108-2   9.95

OPEN HOUSE by Pat Welch. 176 pp. 4th Helen Black Mystery.
ISBN 1-56280-102-3   10.95

ONCE MORE WITH FEELING by Peggy J. Herring. 240 pp.
Lighthearted, loving romantic adventure. ISBN 1-56280-089-2   10.95

FOREVER by Evelyn Kennedy. 224 pp. Passionate romance — love
overcoming all obstacles. ISBN 1-56280-094-9   10.95

WHISPERS by Kris Bruyer. 176 pp. Romantic ghost story
ISBN 1-56280-082-5   10.95

NIGHT SONGS by Penny Mickelbury. 224 pp. 2nd Gianna Maglione
Mystery. ISBN 1-56280-097-3   10.95

GETTING TO THE POINT by Teresa Stores. 256 pp. Classic
southern Lesbian novel. ISBN 1-56280-100-7   10.95

PAINTED MOON by Karin Kallmaker. 224 pp. Delicious
Kallmaker romance. ISBN 1-56280-075-2   10.95

THE MYSTERIOUS NAIAD edited by Katherine V. Forrest &
Barbara Grier. 320 pp. Love stories by Naiad Press authors.
ISBN 1-56280-074-4   14.95

DAUGHTERS OF A CORAL DAWN by Katherine V. Forrest.
240 pp. Tenth Anniversay Edition. ISBN 1-56280-104-X   10.95

BODY GUARD by Claire McNab. 208 pp. 6th Carol Ashton
Mystery. ISBN 1-56280-073-6   10.95

CACTUS LOVE by Lee Lynch. 192 pp. Stories by the beloved
storyteller.   ISBN 1-56280-071-X   9.95

SECOND GUESS by Rose Beecham. 216 pp. 2nd Amanda Valentine
Mystery.   ISBN 1-56280-069-8   9.95

THE SURE THING by Melissa Hartman. 208 pp. L.A. earthquake
romance.   ISBN 1-56280-078-7   9.95

A RAGE OF MAIDENS by Lauren Wright Douglas. 240 pp. 6th Caitlin
Reece Mystery.   ISBN 1-56280-068-X   10.95

TRIPLE EXPOSURE by Jackie Calhoun. 224 pp. Romantic drama
involving many characters.   ISBN 1-56280-067-1   10.95

UP, UP AND AWAY by Catherine Ennis. 192 pp. Delightful
romance.   ISBN 1-56280-065-5   9.95

PERSONAL ADS by Robbi Sommers. 176 pp. Sizzling short
stories.   ISBN 1-56280-059-0   10.95

FLASHPOINT by Katherine V. Forrest. 256 pp. Lesbian
blockbuster!   ISBN 1-56280-043-4   22.95

CROSSWORDS by Penny Sumner. 256 pp. 2nd Victoria Cross
Mystery.   ISBN 1-56280-064-7   9.95

SWEET CHERRY WINE by Carol Schmidt. 224 pp. A novel of
suspense.   ISBN 1-56280-063-9   9.95

CERTAIN SMILES by Dorothy Tell. 160 pp. Erotic short stories.
                                                 ISBN 1-56280-066-3   9.95

EDITED OUT by Lisa Haddock. 224 pp. 1st Carmen Ramirez
Mystery.   ISBN 1-56280-077-9   9.95

WEDNESDAY NIGHTS by Camarin Grae. 288 pp. Sexy
adventure.   ISBN 1-56280-060-4   10.95

SMOKEY O by Celia Cohen. 176 pp. Relationships on the
playing field.   ISBN 1-56280-057-4   9.95

KATHLEEN O'DONALD by Penny Hayes. 256 pp. Rose and
Kathleen find each other and employment in 1909 NYC.
                                                 ISBN 1-56280-070-1   9.95

STAYING HOME by Elisabeth Nonas. 256 pp. Molly and Alix
want a baby . . . or do they?   ISBN 1-56280-076-0   10.95

TRUE LOVE by Jennifer Fulton. 240 pp. Six lesbians searching
for love in all the "right" places.   ISBN 1-56280-035-3   10.95

These are just a few of the many Naiad Press titles — we are the oldest and
largest lesbian/feminist publishing company in the world. We also offer an
enormous selection of lesbian video products. Please request a complete
catalog. We offer personal service; we encourage and welcome direct mail
orders from individuals who have limited access to bookstores carrying our
publications.